The Home Trade of Manchester

MANCHESTER:
EXAMINER PRINTING WORKS,
PALL MALL.

PREFACE.

———

IN the following chapters, bearing directly or indirectly on the Home Trade of Manchester, in one or other of its aspects, and on social and moral considerations, which are of importance to the workers in connection with it, I have but one aim—to create a more hopeful attitude generally, and to add some little inspiration to the efforts which are being so abundantly put forth in our city.

Whether touching upon personal recollections or facts in the life and growth of Manchester, upon the prospects of the home trade, and of Manchester as a great centre of the same, or the leading principles of retail trading, my desire has been to show that there is yet offered scope and reward to the worker who possesses enthusiasm, prudence, and intelligence.

The chapters on the Home-Trade and Commercial

Travellers' Associations, and on some of the Provident and Benevolent Societies, are mainly explanatory of the nature and objects which these associations have in view, but facts and opinions are added, either to illustrate their methods of action or to confirm in the reader's mind the sense of their importance.

The two chapters on "The life and duties of business men" and "To young men" are for the most part of the nature of reflections upon the moral and social aspects and powers of the lives of men engaged in business pursuits, and are included in this volume in the hope that some stimulus may be given in the search for the higher meanings of life, and some craving for usefulness over and above mere success.

The addresses, as will be seen, were nearly all delivered at Crewe at the annual gatherings of the employés of Rylands and Company, at their works there, and treat of general business topics.

The jottings are a series of scraps, cuttings, musings, and otherwise, such as most men who go through life with eyes and heart open to what is passing around them accumulate.

The little volume is quite unpretentious. No great claim for originality is made. Probably the large part of what is written will appear commonplace to men of anything like the experience of Manchester life which the writer has had. Yet, it is written with an earnest purpose—not only to interest, but to help and inspire, and, in some cases even, to guide and counsel the reader. Amongst the members of the Rylands Memorial Club there are men from almost every sphere of our business life, and it is hoped that to many of such the book may be a token of the writer's interest and sympathy, not only in and with the club, but in and with its individual members.

THE AUTHOR.

Manchester,
    December, 1889.

CONTENTS.

The functions of the Manchester Home-Trade Association—Correspondence with the Postmaster-General with
reference to pattern and sample post—Further postal and
telegraphic reforms—Railway facilities for commercial travellers—Petition against the Railway Companies Bills before
Parliament during the session of 1884-85, applying for inor-
dinate powers in connection with terminal charges—Action
with regard to the bankruptcy laws—Memorials to the Board
of Trade—Other parliamentary measures with which the
Manchester Home-Trade Association has been actively
identified—Establishment of a fund, by mutual co-operation,
to cover the expenses attending the prosecution of fraudulent
debtors—Examples of the kind of excuses made by fraudulent debtors with regard to their insolvency—Investigation
of debtors' effects leads to suspicious discoveries—Reference
to the committee of the Home-Trade Association—The
Commercial Travellers' Association—Other functions discharged by commercial travellers in addition to their ordinary
business routine—The scope of the Commercial Travellers'
Association—*The Mail Train* on "Circular Season Tickets"
—Anent charges for parcels left and the amount of luggage
allowed—*Excerpta* from a memorial to the United Meeting
of Representatives of English Railway Companies in 1888—
Reference to the check system and the desirability of separate
luggage compartments for commercial travellers' sample
cases—The reasonableness of the claims urged upon the
railway companies by commercial travellers.

Introductory statement—The Commercial Travellers'
Benevolent Association—Three essential duties incumbent
upon commercial travellers—The Manchester Warehousemen

Business by no means a "hum-drum" condition of
existence—Trade in its comprehensive sphere affords scope
for the highest faculties, intellectually and morally—Complicated problems constantly arising demanding solution—
Banking, insurance, and the art of buying and selling are
matters requiring extremely delicate handling—It is incumbent upon the business man, by word and deed, to afford an
example of conduct which will beneficially influence those
around him—Among other moral responsibilities there is the
duty of identification with the general public interest, both
locally and nationally, especially in matters affecting trade,
among which one of the most important is the education of
the rising generation—The qualifications of a manufacturer
described, as illustrative of the commercial aspect of life and
duty—The life influence covers a much broader ground—
There is a bounden duty for employers of labour to identify
themselves with the domestic well-being of their workpeople,
by co-operating with them in anything calculated to amelio-
rate their social condition—Sir Titus Salt and the late Mr.
John Rylands examples of men who felt that they had
resting upon them the responsibility of the lives and comforts
of those in their employment—Personal character reflected
in the administration of factory or warehouse and the regularity with which business proceeds—The competition of
foreign countries makes it imperative that we train our
workers by technical instruction—The elementary education
the essential preliminary of technical education happily made
compulsory by the nation—The lifelong experience and
reputation of character gained by business men affords a high
qualification, which leads to their invitation to represent the

Interesting incidents in connection with the memorable
event of the great fire which occurred, during the year 1854,
at the warehouse of Rylands and Sons—Remarkable escape
of Mr. William Rylands—The grave apprehensions of the
late Mr. John Rylands, having the firm conviction that his
son had perished in the ruins—Other references to the late
Mr. William Rylands—An anxious night attended by
ludicrous incidents of a harmless character during the
Fenian excitement in November, 1867—Recollections of
Mr. Alderman George Booth and Mr. John Wade—Some
notable events.

THE
HOME TRADE OF MANCHESTER.

CHAPTER I.

THE GROWTH OF MANCHESTER

BAINES, in his work on *Lancashire and Cheshire*, says: " It has required a period of one thousand five hundred to one thousand six hundred years, if not longer, to raise Manchester to what it now is, although nearly three-fourths of its growth has taken place during the present century. The great natural advantage of Manchester, in former times, was the fertile range of country that extends up the river Irwell to Bury, and down the same river to Warrington, together with the abundance of water power supplied by the confluence of the three rivers—Irwell, Irk, and Medlock—within its limits. In modern times, the greatest natural advantage of Manchester has been its position in the immediate neighbourhood of two of the Lancashire coalfields. The upper or Manchester coalfield comes close upon the city and even within it on the east, while the great middle coalfield of Lancashire approaches as near as to Pendleton on the west. It thus possesses and has for ages possessed every advantage as a manufacturing city

B

that nature could supply, and these have been improved
by intelligence, skill, and the most persevering industry.
The original recommendations of the site of Manchester to the Romans, who either founded or greatly
improved the city (which was known in ancient times
as Mamucium or Mancunium), were the fertility of the
soil, the healthiness of the position, and the neighbourhood of rivers, which they used for the purpose of
defence as well as that of communication. These
natural advantages maintained Manchester in existence
during the whole of the Saxon period with the rank
of a burgh or town, which it held in the time of Alfred
the Great and his son, Edward the Elder, 871–925
A.D., even after it had been almost ruined in the wars
between the Danes of Northumberland and the Saxon
kings. At the time of the Domesday survey, Manchester was the most considerable place in south
Lancashire, though at that time much decayed from
the desperate wars that had been waged for so many
hundred years in the north of England. In the year
1222, King Henry III. granted the right to hold a
weekly market and a yearly fair at Manchester, and,
in the year 1301, Thomas de Gresley, baron of Manchester, granted a charter to the burgesses of Manchester, with the usual privileges of local government and
of trade" (vol. i., pp. 188–9).

On the death of the previous baron, Robert de
Gresley, in 1282, his successor, Thomas de Gresley,
being only eleven years of age, became a ward of the
crown during his minority, the king receiving the
rents until the heir attained manhood. Before entering

into occupation, Edward I. required the High Sheriff of Lancashire to make a return of the particulars of the estate of the late baron. The High Sheriff convened a jury of twelve landowners, which in their report stated *inter alia*, "'and there is there rent of assise (or ancient fixed rent) of the burgages in Mamecestre, which pay yearly, at the Nativity of the Lord, at the Annunciation of the Blessed Mary, at the Nativity of St. John the Baptist, and at the Feast of St. Michael, £7. 3s. 2d.' As the rents of the burgages were fixed at a shilling per burgage, it would appear from this statement of rent that the number of burgages, and probably of burgesses, existing in Manchester at that time was a hundred and forty-three; this, allowing for women and children as well as for men, would give a population of from eight hundred to a thousand persons, exclusive of non-burgesses, who would be very likely to be quite as numerous. This is the earliest glimpse that we obtain of the population of Manchester" (vol. i., p. 689).

" Manchester, after a long period of inactivity, began to increase and advance in population, wealth, and trade in the reigns of Henry VII. and Henry VIII. 'One writeth,' says Hollingworth, 'that about 1520 there were three famous clothiers living in the north country, namely, Cuthbert of Kendal, Hodgkins of Halifax, and Martin Brian (some say Byrom) of Manchester. Every one of these kept a great number of servants at work, carders, spinners, weavers, fullers, dyers, shearmen, etcetera, to the great admiration of those that came into their houses to behold them.' It was at this time that the inhabitants of Manchester induced Parliament to pass an act abolishing the right of sanctuary in Manchester, and removing that dangerous and mischievous privilege to Chester. The following extract from the preamble of the act will show what was the position of the trade of Manchester at this period :—

"Whereas, the said towne of Manchester is, and hath of long tyme been, a towne well inhabited; and the kinge's subjectes inhabitauntes of the same towne are well set a worke in makinge of clothes, as well of lynnen as of woollen, whereby the inhabitauntes of the said towne have obteyned, gotten, and come unto riches and wealthy lyvings, and have kepte and set manye artificers and poore folkes to worke within the same towne; and by reason of the great occupienge, good order, strayte and true dealinge of the inhabitauntes of the said towne, many strangers, as well of Ireland as of other places within this realme, have resorted to the said towne with lynnen yarns, woolles, and other necessary wares for making of clothes, to be sold there, and have used to credit and truste the poore inhabitauntes of the same towne which were not able and had not redy money to pay in hande for the saide yarns, woolles, and wares, unto such time the said credites with their industry, labour, and peynes myght make clothes of the said woolles, yarns, and other necessary wares, and solde the same, to contente and pay their creditours; wherein hath consisted much of the common welthe of the same towne, and many poore folkes had lyving, and children and servants were vertuously brought up in honest and true labour, out of all ydleness. And for as muche as of necessitie the said lynnen yarne must lie about, as well in the night as in the day, continually forthe space of one halfe yere to be whited before it can be made clothe, and the woollen clothes there made must hange uppon the taynter to be dried before it can be dressed up; and for the saulfegarde thereof it is and shal be expedient and necessary that substantiall, honest, true, and credible persons be and shuld dwell in the said towne, and no maner of lyght persone or persons there to be inhabitauntes. And whereas manye straungers, inhabytinge in other towneshyps and places, have used customably to resort to the sayd towne of Manchester with a great number of cottons to be uttered and sold to the inhabitauntes of the same towne, to the great profit of all the inhabitauntes of the same; and thereby many poore people have been well set a worke, as well with dressyng and frisyng of the sayd cottons as with putting to sale the same, &c.— Act 33 Henry VIII." (vol. i., p. 694).

"In the reign of Henry VIII., Leland, the famous antiquary, visited Manchester on his journey through England under the commission granted to him by the king. He informs us in his *Itinerary* that he rode over the Mersey water by a great bridge of timber (then, probably, the old bridge at Stretford), and then over Medlock river, and so within a mile of Manchester. He describes Manchester as the 'fairest, best builded, quickest (busiest), and most populous town in all Lancashire, though with only one parish church; that, however, collegiate, double-aisled, and built of the hardest cut stone.' He speaks of the manufacturers of Manchester as 'buying much Irish yarn at Liverpool.' There were several stone bridges in the town; the best of these crossed the river Irwell, 'that divides Manchester from Salford, which is a large suburb of Manchester.' On this bridge there was then a pretty chapel. The next bridge was that over the Irk river, 'on which the fair builded college standeth, as in the very point of the mouth of it.' On the Irk were divers 'fair mills, that served the town.' In the town, he says, were two fair market-places, and about two flight shottes without the town, beneath, on the same Irwell, are 'yet to be seen dikes and foundations of old Man-castel in a ground now enclosed.' The stones of the ruins of this castle were used for building the bridges of the town. 'It is not long,' says Leland, 'since the church of Manchester was collegiated. The town of Manchester standeth on a hard rock of stone, else Irwell, as well appeareth on the left bank, had been mischievous to the town'" (vol. i., p. 696).

"Aston, in his *Manchester Guide*, gives an illustration of the manners of this time in the form of an inventory of the personal habiliments and furniture of a widow, residing at Salford, in the year 1588. The widow's clothes consisted of a trained gown lined with camlet, a cassock, frieze gowns, a worsted kirtle with branched damask body and sleeves; a russet taffety kirtle and apron, silk hats, a tammy mantle, a golden girdle, partlets, smocks, cross clothes, and mufflers. The clothes of the widow's late husband comprised 'a myllom (Milan) fustian doublet, oylypoyld sleeves, breeches, a pair of moulds, a frieze jerkin, two sealskin girdles, two pair round hose, a felt hat and band, and a dagger.' The deceased had been a manufacturer of frieze" (vol. i., p. 698).

About this time, *i.e.*, in the reign of Queen Elizabeth, Camden speaks of Manchester " as excelling all the neighbouring towns in ornament, populousness, in its woollen manufacture, its court-house, church, and college," and speaks of the superiority of its woollen cloths, then known by the name of " Manchester cottons." These manufactures were known in the Brazils in the year 1573. In the reign of James I., cotton wool began to be imported into Manchester from the Levant; and, in the reign of Charles II., Andrew Yarranton, one of the principal writers on trade of that age, spoke of Manchester as being " the great master in all things that it trades in."

GROWTH OF MANCHESTER AND DEVELOPMENT OF COTTON TRADE DURING SEVENTEENTH CENTURY.

The growth of Manchester and the combination of influences rendering that growth possible during the eighteenth century may be traced *seriatim* in the order of their development as follows:—

1701. Carlyle, in his *Past and Present*, gives an effective contrast of the condition of England in the twelfth century with the activity of the nineteenth century. It may in truth be said to be a tolerably fair description of the condition of the country at the end of the seventeenth century, five centuries later: "How silent lie all cotton trades and such like; not a steeple chimney yet got on end from sea to sea! The Ribble and the Aire roll down as yet unpolluted by dyers' chemistry; tenanted by the merry trouts and piscatory otters; the sunbeam and the vacant wind's-blast alone traversing those moors. Side by side sleep the coal strata and the iron strata for so many ages. No steam demon has yet risen smoking into being. . . . Mancunium, Manceaster, what we now call Manchester, spins no cotton—if it be not wool 'cottons' clipped from the backs of mountain sheep. The creek of the Mersey gurgles, twice in the four and twenty hours, with eddying brine clangorous with sea-fowl, and is a *Lither* Pool, a *lazy* or Sullen Pool, no monstrous pitchy city and sea-haven of the world!"

At the beginning of the thirteenth century King John, after the partial conquest of Ireland by Strongbow, finding that a creek or pool existed on the Lancashire shore of the Mersey estuary would afford a

superior haven for embarkation to Ireland than Shot-
wick on the Dee, about six miles below Chester, which
Richard I. at the end of the twelfth century had
selected with the same object in view and had built a
castle for its protection, laid out a small town, erected
one hundred and sixty-eight burgage tenements, and
by letters patent granted certain privileges to his subjects to settle there.   This new settlement under royal
patronage was called Liverpul.   The king built a
castle there.   Liverpool was, however, merely held to
be a creek of the port of Chester.   It fully answered
the purpose for which it was founded, though five centuries elapsed before it became of any degree of importance.   In 1701, an old record states that "the
town of Liverpool rises rapidly into importance and
first forms the port of Manchester."   The geographical
situation of Liverpool in relation to the extensive industrial districts of South Lancashire, the West Riding
of Yorkshire, and the county of Chester, the manufactures of which were expanding at a rapid rate, made
it the natural avenue of the egress from and the ingress
to the "hinterland" for its sea-borne traffic requirements.   The imports of cotton into this country in
that year (1701), chiefly through London from Smyrna,
was 886 tons, the official values of the exports of cotton
goods being £33,253.

1721. On June 6th of this year, the Mersey and
Irwell Navigation between Manchester and Liverpool
was opened for the passage of vessels of 50 tons
burden.

1730. In this year John Wyatt, of Birmingham, spun

the first cotton yarn made in England by machinery, the method being the rollers system.

1738. The system of cotton spinning by means of rollers was further improved by John Wyatt, which was patented in the name of his partner, Lewis Paul. In the same year John Kay, a loom-maker, of Colchester, patented the fly-shuttle, reducing the labour of weaving by one-half. This unfortunate inventor died in poverty and obscurity in Paris, no stone indicating where he lies. Efforts were made to obtain an adequate reward from the Government for the benefits he had conferred upon his countrymen, but these efforts were fruitless.

1740. At this time the agency system had come into operation, and the weaving of cotton had been considerably extended. The custom at this time was for Manchester merchants to give out warps and raw cotton to the weavers, receiving them back in cloth, and paying for the carding, roving, spinning, and weaving. The weaving of a piece containing twelve pounds of eighteen-penny weft occupied a weaver about fourteen days, receiving for the weaving eighteen shillings; spinning the weft at ninepence per pound, nine shillings; picking, carding, and roving, eight shillings.

1743. Up to this time East India yarns had been used in Lancashire for the manufacture of fine goods.

1748. In this year Lewis Paul took out a second patent for the carding of wool and cotton by means of a revolving cylinder.

1752. The dock dues paid on vessels at the port of Liverpool amounted to £1,776.

1756. In this year cotton velvets were first made at Bolton. The first enumeration of the population of Manchester and Salford showed the number of inhabitants to be nineteen thousand eight hundred and thirty-nine.

1757. The dock dues paid at the port of Liverpool, on one thousand three hundred and seventy-one vessels, amounted to £2,337.

1758. The patent of Lewis Paul for spinning with rollers was renewed.

1759. Great improvements were effected by Mr. Mather in the manufacture of ginghams, damasks, and moreens, also in the dyeing processes. Manchester begins to have an excellent reputation for its cotton manufactures, the value of the goods made amounting to £200,000 per annum. A weaver's cottage, with a two-loom shop, rented at forty to forty-five shillings a year.

1760. The drop box invented by Robert Kay, of Bury, a son of the inventor of the fly-shuttle. By means of this invention the weaver can at pleasure use any one of three shuttles, each containing a differently coloured weft, without the trouble of taking them from and replacing on the lathe or slay.

1761. The Bridgewater Canal, from Worsley to Castlefield, Knot Mill, Manchester, seven and three-quarter miles in length, was opened for traffic. The illustrious Duke of Bridgewater employed the genius of Brindley, the object of his grace being to develop his extensive collieries at Worsley, by affording cheapness for the coals required in Manchester. Besides the great saving effected by the cheapness of coals to domestic consumers, which the Worsley canal made possible, the price being only one-fourth of that they had hitherto been sold at, that waterway also provided the cheap fuel upon which it soon afterwards came to pass that the future of the cotton manufacture mainly depended.

1762. The secret of turkey red dyeing introduced by John Wilson, of Ainsworth.

1763. First cotton quiltings made by Joseph Shaw, of Bolton. British muslins, both striped and plain, first manufactured by Mr. Shaw, at Anderton, near Chorley. The first spinning jenny constructed by Thomas Highs, a reed maker, at Leigh, in Lancashire, the machine being so named after his favourite daughter, Jane. However meritorious may have been subsequent improvements, Thomas Highs was the inceptor of a development of cotton machinery which led to its diffusion throughout the industrial world.

1764. At this time the trade of Manchester was greatly pushed by the practice of sending outriders for orders throughout the country, carrying patterns with them in bags. The imports of raw cotton during this year amounted to one thousand seven hundred and twenty-eight tons; the exports of cotton goods being, according to official values, £200,354. The dock dues paid at the port of Liverpool, on one thousand six hundred and twenty-five vessels, amounted to £2,780.

1767. James Hargreaves, a weaver, of Standhill, near Blackburn, who has been called "one of the martyrs of scientific industry," improved upon the spinning jenny,

the device of Thomas Highs, of Bolton.   He was also
the inventor of the crank and comb, which facilitated
the carding of cotton.   He was compelled to leave the
place of his nativity owing to the cry of "Men, not
machines."   He died in Nottingham workhouse, in
1777, having had his machinery destroyed, his patent
invaded, and his prospects blighted.

1769. In this year Richard Arkwright, who was
born in Preston in 1732, took out his first patent for
making mule yarn by means of rollers, and built a
mill at Nottingham.   The invention in its perfected
form may be assigned to the year 1771.   It is known
as the water frame, and gave the name to water twist.
The idea of the machine patented by Arkwright was
as follows: A soft ribbon of cotton wool, technically
known as a sliver, becomes flattened by passing
between two revolving cylinders, the lower one fluted,
the other being sheathed in leather, thence passing
between a second pair of rollers revolving at a much
greater rate, and is thus elongated and hardened into
a firmer thread.   In 1776 Arkwright obtained a further
patent for carding, drawing, and roving frames.   The
history of Richard Arkwright is a romance.   The
thirteenth blessing of the family of a Preston opera-
tive, by his twenty-eighth year is found to have
developed into an ingenious and persevering barber,
occupying a cellar in Bolton, during the year 1760
carrying on a fierce competition with others of his
craft, having a sign hung outside his door inscribed
"Richard Arkwright, Subterranean Barber—a Clean
Shave for a Halfpenny."   The original model of

the water frame of Arkwright now forms an interesting relic in the South Kensington Museum. In 1786, the Bolton barber received as a distinguished inventor and extensive cotton spinner the honour of knighthood. Sir Richard Arkwright became the High Sheriff of Derbyshire, and died at Cromford in 1792, in his sixtieth year, leaving a fortune of over half a million, which was trebled by his son. This remarkable character at fifty years of age devoted two hours daily in learning how to write and acquiring the rudiments of grammar.

While Richard Arkwright had been pondering over his spinning frame, the genius of the celebrated James Watt was engaged upon the perfection of the steam-engine. It was on January 5th, 1769, the same year in which Arkwright obtained his patent for his spinning machine, that James Watt took out his patent for his steam, or, as he called it, fire engine. Then steam began to roll the spindles and work the reeds at an astonishing rate, multiplying the produce of the factories beyond anticipation. Spinning and weaving, which had been hitherto domestic operations, under the factory system enabled all the processes of manufacture to be combined under one roof, and enabled also a rigid sub-division of labour. In this wise Lancashire has come to be able to clothe the world at ridiculously low prices. James Watt was born in Greenock in 1736, and died in 1819. He commenced life as a mathematical instrument maker. The action of steam as a motive power was known before the Christian era. Hero of Alexandria, who lived in

B.C. 285–222, describes an instrument termed the
æolipile, consisting of a globular metallic vessel resting
on points where it revolves with facility. The pivots
are the extremities of tubes from a boiler underneath,
bent at right angles, shut at the extremities, but with
a small aperture at the side where the steam may
escape, and forces the globe in the opposite direction.
The ancient æolipile, the fire-water work of the Marquis
of Worcester in 1663, the steam-engine of Savery in
1698, and that of Newcomen and Cawley, 1713, known
as the atmospheric engine, all of which Watt justly
described as merely "fine playthings," never brought
steam power within the range of practicability, it being
left to Watt to bring the steam-engine within an ace
of finality in perfection by disciplining this natural force,
art thus subjecting nature to control.   But for an Act
of Parliament obtained in 1775, extending the patent
rights of Watt until 1800 in consideration of the great
utility of the invention, the inventor must have been
entirely deprived of the reward of his labour.

1770. During this year Richard Arkwright built a
mill at Cromford in Derbyshire.   Great improvements
in the manufacture of ginghams effected by the inven-
tions of Mr. Meadowcroft.

1772. John Kay, junior, of Bury, a son of the inventor of the fly-shuttle, received an honorarium of
two hundred guineas from the cotton manufacturers
of Manchester for his invention of the double jenny,
which was exhibited in the Exchange.   In this year
John Lees, a Quaker, of Manchester, invented the
feeder used in the manufacture of cotton.

1773. The manufacture of calicoes introduced about this time. An enumeration of the population of Manchester and Salford shows the number of inhabitants to be twenty-five thousand one hundred and thirty-six, and that of the out-townships to be thirteen thousand seven hundred and eighty-six, making a general total of thirty-eight thousand nine hundred and twenty-two.

1774. In this year an Act of Parliament, imposing a duty on printed, painted, and stained cottons, declares the manufacture to be lawful! *O tempora! O mores!*

1776. This year is distinguished by the opening of the Runcorn branch of the Bridgewater Canal system, on March 21st, in that year. The most noble Francis Egerton, Duke of Bridgewater, being eminently satisfied with the success attending his first adventure, the Worsley Canal, obtained the sanction of the legislature to construct a canal from Waters Meeting—a point on the Worsley Canal, three miles and a quarter from the terminal wharves at Castlefield, Knot Mill, Manchester—to the port of Runcorn, on the Mersey estuary, the length of the navigation between Waters Meeting and Runcorn being twenty-five and a half miles. This important system of navigation, which, including an extension of the Worsley Canal to Leigh, makes the total length of navigation thirty-nine and three-quarter miles. The Bridgewater Canals undertaking was acquired, along with the Mersey and Irwell Navigation, by the Manchester Ship Canal Company for the sum of £1,710,000, by the payment of a single cheque on August 3rd, 1887. The volume of traffic conveyed during the year 1888 amounted, according to the return made to the Board of Trade, in pursuance of section 39, sub-section 2 of the Railway and Canal Traffic Act, 1888, to two million nine hundred and sixteen thousand seven hundred and fifty-four tons, the net revenue being £71,937, showing £4·42 per cent on the total capital of £1,710,000. This canals system is in direct connection with the Weaver Navigation, the Trent and Mersey, Rochdale, and Leeds and Liverpool Canals, and forms the avenue to and from the Mersey for the Ashton, Oldham, and Stockport, Peak Forest, Macclesfield, and Huddersfield Canals, and the Calder and Hebble and Aire and Calder Navigations, thus affording access between the east and west coasts and the intervening district, comprising Lancashire, the West Riding of Yorkshire, also Cheshire, Derbyshire, and North Staffordshire.

1777. Green dye for cotton goods invented by R. Williams.

1779. Samuel Crompton, a weaver, of Hall-in-the-Wood, near Bolton, invented the spinning mule. His mother, a widow, kept him hard at work at the loom. Crompton, however, being much fonder of his fiddle than the loom, grew impatient at the breaking of the threads, which seriously disturbed him in his musical propensity. He, therefore, resolved to experiment in order to ascertain whether anything could be devised in order to expedite his work. He worked in secret for five years in the night time after his labour for the day in weaving was done. In addition to his occupation as a weaver, he supplemented his income by performing in the orchestra at the Bolton Theatre with his violin, for which he received eighteenpence per night. This enabled him to purchase tools and materials with which he worked away, until at last, after infinite toil, he had finished his "mule," this name being given because it is a sort of cross between the spinning machine of Arkwright and Hargreaves' jenny. Perceval, the Premier, had promised Crompton that he would propose a grant of £20,000 by the Government in recognition of his services. The assassination of Perceval, however, prevented the fulfilment of his promise. A grant was, however, made by the Government of £5,000. This sum was scarcely adequate to cover his debts and losses, and utterly inadequate in relation to the public benefit accruing from his invention, and ungenerous on the part of a Government receiving more than £1,000 a working day in respect of a duty levied on the imports of raw cotton eventually being spun on the machines he had invented. Samuel Crompton was born in 1753, and died in his seventy-fourth year in 1827, adding another name to the list of those who have suffered martyrdom in the cause of art.

1780. The manufacture of muslins introduced. The imports of raw cotton amounted to 3,100 tons. The exports of cotton goods officially valued at £355,000.

1782. It is interesting to note that in this year it is recorded that a panic was created in Manchester owing to the importation of seven thousand bags of cotton, between December and April. In this year the legislature sanctioned a statute prohibiting the exportation of engraved copper plates and blocks in connection with calico printing, and imposing a penalty of £100

C

with the alternative of twelve months' imprisonment for enticing any workman engaged in calico printing to go beyond the seas.

1784. The legislature during this year sanctioned a measure imposing a duty, usually referred to as the Fustian Tax, of one penny per yard upon all bleached cotton manufactures. Fifteen houses, employing thirty-eight thousand hands, petitioned against it, and the master bleachers and dyers announced that, "they would be under the sad necessity of declining their present occupation till the next session of Parliament." In order to obtain the repeal of this obnoxious measure two of the principal merchants of Manchester, Mr. Thomas Walker and Mr. Thomas Richardson, were deputed, at the opening of the next session of Parliament, to wait on Mr. William Pitt, who was the First Lord of the Treasury, in his capacity of Chancellor of the Exchequer, then holding the two portfolios. Their representations, supported as they were by petitions from the various manufacturing towns, and aided by the powerful influence of the Duke of Bridgewater, enabled the attainment of their object, the repeal of the tax on the cotton industry. Both gentlemen were presented with silver cups, and splendid processions were made in celebration of their successful efforts. Mr. William Pitt, the Premier, estimated the number employed in the cotton trade generally at that time as eighty thousand.

The year 1784 was also characterised by the adventitious circumstance which led Dr. Edmund Cartwright to invent the power loom. This *littérateur* had had nothing in the course of his life to suggest the remotest possibility of his ever being included in the list of distinguished mechanical inventors. Being at Matlock in the summer of 1784, he incidentally fell in with some gentlemen of Manchester, when, in the course of conversation, reference was made to the spinning machinery of Arkwright. One of the company observed that as soon as the patent of Arkwright expired, so many spinning mills would be erected, and such an output of yarn, hands could not possibly be found to weave it. Dr. Cartwright said that, in such an event, Arkwright must then set his wits to work to invent a weaving mill. The company generally were of opinion that the thing was impracticable. Dr. Cartwright, however, was convinced that the idea was feasible. Being endowed with herculean strength of resolve, he devoted all his time, energy, and resources to the evolution of a practicable means of accomplishing his object. His literary pursuits were abandoned, and, employing carpenter and smith, in the course of six months he produced a clumsy-looking specimen of mechanism as the result of his lucubrations, which, however, contained the embryo of the power loom. This crude stage of his power loom he secured by patent on April 4th, 1785. In its primitive form the loom was impracticable. However, after actual observation of the working of the looms then in existence, he was enabled to complete his invention after a couple of years' further pondering, and obtained his last patent on August 1st, 1787. In that year he established a weaving and spinning factory at Doncaster. He suffered greatly from the usual troubles which afflicted the inventors of labour-saving machinery—the hostility of the operatives, under the impression that they would lose their livelihood; and the equally vexatious and unjustifiable infringements on patent rights, by rival manufacturers, involving costly litigation; and by insidious corruption enticing from his employment the most efficient of his workmen. Notwithstanding he had expended his fortune, and, finally, his pen alone left him as a means of subsistence, he went on inventing until the day of his death. To record these would require a portly volume. In 1808, when Perceval was the Chancellor of the Exchequer, Parliament made him a grant of £10,000, which saved him from want or the need of toil during the evening of his life. Edmund Cartwright was born at Marnham, in Nottinghamshire, in 1743, and passed away, in the eighty-fifth year of his age, in 1827.

1787. An Act of Parliament passed for the encouragement of the art of designing original patterns for prints. Steam-engines first used in Lancashire factories by Messrs. Peel at Warrington. The muslin manufacture greatly increases through mule spinning, the production amounting to five hundred thousand pieces per annum. Owing to the lapse of the patent of Arkwright in 1785, the official valuation of the exports of cotton goods in 1787 amounted to £1,101,457.

1788. Cotton manufacture estimated to employ one hundred and fifty-nine thousand men, ninety thousand women, and one hundred children. East Indian and North American raw cotton first imported. Depression in cotton trade referred to importation of East Indian goods, the Government being solicited to allow a drawback as a stimulant of the export of home productions. The population of Manchester and Salford enumerated as fifty thousand persons; total number of families, ten thousand; number of houses inhabited, seven thousand one hundred and seventy-six.

1789. Steam power for spinning cotton first applied in Manchester by Mr. Drinkwater.

1790. Imports of raw cotton amounted to 14,000 tons, the official valuation of exports of cotton goods being £1,662,339. Manchester paid in postages £11,000, being a larger amount than any other provincial town.

1800. The imports of raw cotton amounted to twenty-five thousand tons. The official valuation of exports of cotton goods being £5,406,501. The dock duties paid on four thousand seven hundred and forty-six vessels, with an aggregate tonnage of 450,060, amounted to £23,380.

GROWTH OF MANCHESTER AND DEVELOPMENT OF COTTON INDUSTRY DURING THE NINETEENTH CENTURY.

During the nineteenth century, the manifold developments in the methods of production, the means of distribution, and the facilities for intercommunication, have been so numerous as to prevent the possibility of a further description than a brief summary of the influences which, during the nine decades of this century, have combined to make Manchester the next community in rank to London in its metropolitan qualifications. Among these influences were the interesting labours of Richard Trevethick, John Blenkinsop, William Hedley, and Timothy Hackworth, which, with the great triumph of George Stephenson—the construction of the Liverpool and Manchester Railway—initiated an era of unexampled progress, which has extended over a period exceeding half a century. Simultaneously with the efforts of the persistent and ingenious minds which had so vastly improved methods of production and distribution, enlightened statesmen had devoted their energies to the deletion from our statutes of some of the impolitic restrictions which had seriously hampered the legitimate progress of industrial development. These legislative reforms have greatly contributed to the expansion of our world-wide commerce. Every agency which lessens the difficulties opposed to the intercommunication of mankind helps by so much the general progress of the human race. In the enormous development of the interests of this country generally, and of Manchester interests particularly, the varied applications of the electric telegraph, and the postal reforms initiated by Sir Rowland Hill, have contributed in an immeasurable degree. The combined operation of mechanical improvements, the inception of ocean steam navigation, scientific research, moral reforms, and improved means of internal communication, have each played a material part in the developments which have made Manchester the greatest workshop of the world, and the commercial metropolis of a population as great as that of Holland and Belgium combined, inhabiting a considerably less area than those countries taken together. No better register of the growth of Manchester can be found than the following figures exhibiting the increase of the commerce of Liverpool, which is simply a reflex of the prosperity of the great industrial area of which Manchester is the commercial emporium.

THE DEVELOPMENT OF LIVERPOOL COMMERCE.

Year.	Number of vessels.	Aggregate tonnage of vessels.	Mean tonnage.	Dock rates and town dues.
1801 ...	5,060 ...	459,719 ...	98 ...	£28,365
1811 ...	5,616 ...	611,190 ...	109 ...	54,752
1821 ...	7,810 ...	839,848 ...	113 ...	94,556
1831 ...	12,537 ...	1,592,436 ...	127 ...	183,455
1841 ...	16,108 ...	2,425,461 ...	150 ...	175,506
1851 ...	21,071 ...	3,737,666 ...	177 ...	246,686
1861 ...	21,095 ...	4,977,272 ...	236 ...	611,006
1871 ...	20,121 ...	6,131,745 ...	305 ...	789,031
1881 ...	20,249 ...	7,893,948 ...	390 ...	966,281
1889 ...	22,662 ...	9,291,964 ...	410 ...	990,552*

The Customs tonnage returns for the year 1889 are—inward, 8,586,381 tons; outward, 8,307,442 tons; total, 16,893,823 tons; number of vessels entered and clearing, 43,443. The weight of the traffic carried would amount to 20,000,000 tons approximately.

---

* The small increase in the amount of revenue, as compared with the marked increase in the volume of tonnage, is referable to reductions in the port charges made by the Mersey Docks and Harbour Board, these reductions being mainly attributable to the moral influence of the Manchester Ship Canal, having been made since the inception of the movement in 1882.

The expansion of Manchester during the sixty years of the railway era, which had its inception in a practicable sense by the opening of the first Liverpool and Manchester railway, on September 15th, 1830, has been truly remarkable. This is evidenced by the subjoined figures, giving the accretion of population in the five poor-law districts of Manchester, Chorlton, Salford, Barton, and Prestwich, which constitute in the aggregate one homogeneous community. The figures are taken from the census returns made for the respective periods:—

1831.	1851.	1871.	1891.
284,238	471,382	643,801	954,808*

The progress of our nation in wealth and commercial prosperity during the last fifty years is marvellous. The population has increased by eleven and a half millions; the imports of the country have increased by £300,000,000; the revenue has gone up from £55,000,000 to £90,000,000; and, as was proved in the

* Calculated on basis of known increase between 1871 and 1881, which was one hundred and thirty-eight thousand four hundred and twenty-nine, or twenty-two per cent, the population in that year being seven hundred and eighty-two thousand six hundred and thirty. Manchester as a community ranks next in population to London. A general impression exists that Glasgow and Liverpool have precedence in this respect before Manchester. As, however, at Midsummer, 1889, there were resident within twelve miles of the Manchester Royal Exchange two million inhabitants, the number in a similar radius around the Glasgow and Liverpool Royal Exchanges being respectively in each case one million, this contention is effectively disposed of. As a matter of fact, within six miles of the Manchester Royal Exchange there is a population of one million, equal to that within twelve miles around the Glasgow or Liverpool Royal Exchanges.

evidence of the Manchester Ship Canal advocates, the shipping has advanced from nine million tons to more than sixty million tons. The postage has made perhaps the most extraordinary leaps, having now reached the prodigious figures: one thousand five hundred million letters annually, five thousand million newspapers and books, one thousand eight hundred million post cards. The income of the country has risen to over £600,000,000, which in itself shows how greatly our command of the comforts and conveniences of life has increased. This is true as much, if not more, of the labouring population as of the middle and higher classes. The wider distribution of wealth, the cheapness of food and clothing, better and more general education, have all tended to bring within the reach of every class comforts and enjoyments undreamed of before; increased longevity is one of the most marked results, as may be seen from our insurance office statistics.

Manchester has admittedly played its part in the general progress. When the writer came to the town in 1845, the population of Manchester was not more than two hundred and fifty thousand, and that of Salford about fifty thousand. In both boroughs the growth has been remarkable, but especially in what is now known as greater Manchester, which takes in the population within a radius of four miles from the Royal Exchange, which is mainly, one might almost say entirely, dependent upon Manchester. The population of this wider area is over eight hundred thousand, and is constantly increasing. At the earlier date many of our well-to-do men lived in George Street, Faulkner Street, and Portland Street. The property adjoining the Queen's Hotel, on which now stand three or four magnificent warehouses, was let as boarding-houses, behind which stood the Fever Hospital. Lever Street was all house property, and also a large part of Oldham Street. Piccadilly was then much narrower, and unadorned by the bronze statues which to-day arrest the attention of every visitor and receive a full measure of consideration at the hands of our juvenile population, who keep them, towards the base at least, well polished. By the way, why should not one of the vacant places at either end of the Piccadilly esplanade be occupied by a statue to the good and great John Bright?

Speaking of the narrow thoroughfares of old Manchester, who that remembers the Tib Street of former days does not pay his tribute of gratitude to the Corporation for the vast improvement that has been made at a very moderate cost? For many years the occupants of warehouses in the neighbourhood had been trying to secure the alteration, which was at last brought about in a curious way. After long agitation, Mr. Alderman Nicholls, who was at that time chairman of the Improvement Committee, was induced to visit the district. He had only gone a few yards up Tib Street from Market Street, when he saw a lurry from one of the side streets turning into Tib Street, and coming in the direction opposite to that in which he was going. He was greatly disconcerted to find that there was only a space of a few inches between the loaded lurry and the buildings. The worthy alderman was driven to do what many hundreds had had to do before, viz., hasten for safety into the open doorway of one of the warehouses. Being assured that this was only an hourly occurrence, he readily promised his support in the negociations for the widening of the thoroughfare; the necessary properties were bought, and now, instead of a lot of dingy old properties, which were a disgrace to the district, we have an important thoroughfare occupied by some well-known houses, and yielding a much larger revenue to the Corporation.

About the time referred to (1845), Messrs. James Brown, Son, and Co., were in Cannon Street; Messrs. S. and J. Watts and Co. in Fountain Street; Messrs. E. and J. Jackson in Mosley Street, at the corner of York Street, where the noble edifice belonging to the Manchester and Salford Banking Company now stands. At the opposite corner stood the old and well-known linen house of Blackwell's. The latter left the trade, but Messrs. Jackson occupied for some time the substantial building next to the Queen's Hotel, now in the occupation of the well-known firm of Richardson, Tee, and Rycroft. Messrs. Kershaw, Lees, and Co. occupied the adjoining warehouse, having removed from the building they had so long occupied in High Street. Messrs. Barbour Bros., having built their palatial warehouse in Aytoun Street, and left their old place in Portland Street, Messrs. J. F. and H. Roberts came from Birchin Lane, and built their new premises on a site at the corner of Portland Street and Aytoun Street. Within a short period of the time we refer to, Portland Street had been occupied very largely by a poor class of property. But shortly after this date it rose in character almost at a bound, and has become a great centre of the commercial power of our city and has in it properties which would be a credit to any town.

High Street is another thoroughfare, which has considerably improved, and, in addition to the three piles of buildings occupied by Rylands and Sons Limited, it has in it other enterprising firms, and the future of this street will be greater than the past.

Some large houses have continued to develop on and around the ground they have for many years occupied in Church Street. This street is still improving in style of buildings, but there is room for further progress in this direction. The writer hopes to live to see the time when the whole length of the street, from High Street to Ducie Street, will be known as Church Street, and will be occupied by strong concerns, which will do their share in the further development of this vast centre for the distribution of the varied and ever-increasing manufactures of Lancashire and Yorkshire.

Old Market Street, formerly called Market Stead Lane or Market Street Lane, was a very different thoroughfare from that we are accustomed to look upon to-day. Then, Newall's Buildings occupied the site which is now covered by the magnificent pile of buildings known as the Royal Exchange. A little above, on the opposite side, was Brooks' Bank, and, further on, a number of poor buildings where now are splendid shops with warehouses or offices above. In walking up the street, one came next to the pile, known as Egyptian Buildings, at the end of which was the old Angel Hotel, with miserable property adjoining; the present substantial stone structures, erected on the same spot, constitute another mark of the splendid improvement which has been in progress. Opposite, on part of the ground now occupied by Lewis's fine premises, stood the Talbot Hotel. Across the street from this point was the entrance to Tib Street, at one corner of which was the well-known and much-frequented Mee's Café. At the other corner was a chemist's shop, occupied by Mr. Standring, a gentleman who had made himself as celebrated and respected as his neighbours, Messrs. Jewsbury and Brown. The fine stone edifice now at the corner of Tib Street, the upper portion of which has for many years been occupied by Rylands and Sons, was built and first occupied by the family of Silvesters. A few yards above this, the building known as the White Bear Hotel was at one time occupied by a Mr. Lever, who owned the lands adjoining. The writer remembers Mr. Rylands telling him of the difficulty there was for two conveyances to pass at the upper part of Market Street, near the corner of High Street, the ground being very high, and the street narrow. There stood at the top of the street a house, *surrounded by a garden*, in the occupation of a Mrs. Thomas Potter. This property was afterwards sold by auction. The advertisement of the sale ran as follows: "To be sold by auction, at the Bridgewater Arms Inn, Manchester, on the 15th September, 1814, all that plot of land extending in length to the front of Mosley

Street, 44 yards and 36 inches, and to the front of Market Street, 32 yards and 8 inches, to the back co-extensive with Back Mosley Street, 45 yards and 24 inches, and to the front of Meal Street, 23 yards and 31 inches, and containing in the whole 1,432 superficial square yards of land, and also the dwelling house, coach house, stables, and offices, and other erections now standing on the same plot; the above premises will be sold subject to an annual ground rent of £47. 14s. 8d.; adjoining the yard is a spacious garden surrounded by a wall and comprising nearly half the above-mentioned land." In the deeds of a property situate in Tib Street the right is *still* reserved to the owner of fishing in the river Tib; and the property is described as the house situate near Carpenter's Lane, having in the front a garden sloping down to the bank of the river Tib, and containing so many square yards of land. And but recently the writer was talking to a gentleman, who had himself fished in the Medlock, near Oxford Road, and taken beautiful trout of it.

Another item is noteworthy, the change in our city architecture generally being characterised by great improvements. One would specially enumerate among these the palatial Town Hall, the Assize Courts, the Royal Exchange, the General Post Office in Spring Gardens, which ranks next in the magnitude of its business to that of St. Martin le Grand in the metropolis, and includes in its function the postal economy of over one hundred towns; the Owens College, the seat of the Victoria University, the Grammar School the Exchange Station, the magnificent warehouses, and most recently numerous new insurance and bank buildings. These all have done much to elevate the character of the city, and impart to it a picturesqueness which makes it attractive to visitors from a distance, and a joy to those of us who are proud to call ourselves citizens of Manchester. The improvement in the Consolidated Bank Buildings, the erection of the new Manchester and County, Manchester Joint Stock, and the Lancashire and Yorkshire Banks have added greatly to the architecture of King Street, and indeed we might say of the city; and now we have the commencement of yet another, the National Provincial Bank in York Street, which, judging from the beautiful and elegant design, and the extent of ground to be covered, will be worthy of the great and wealthy corporation in whose interest it is being erected. It was remarked some time ago by an Italian statesman and writer, who had returned to his own country: " If you want to know what architecture is, and living architecture, you must go to Manchester."

The story of the development of a great town is always interesting and sometimes very remarkable. Conversation with an old inhabitant frequently affords both amusement and instruction. One is urged to reflect what circumstances have caused the current of trade to flow in this or in that direction; why the land in one thoroughfare should be valued at £30 or £50 per yard, whilst in another street, which at a period one can remember would have been considered by many shrewd people as one of the best investments for the future, it has actually gone down in value; why

one side of a thoroughfare is so much more valuable
than the other, so that, in some instances, a moderate
shop worth £300 on one side of the street will be
worth £500 or more directly opposite. Or, again,
taking a given locality that is purely residential, but
where by the increase of population a necessity has
arisen for shops, why does this or that street take the
preference apart altogether from any desire or opinion
of the landlord ?   It is interesting, too, to notice how
the extension of business premises over a wider area
diminishes the value of house property up to a certain
point, which we will call the middle of the three zones
in which the property of a city is situate, so that houses
formerly let at £80 and £100 per annum fall in value
till it becomes difficult to let them at £30 or £40; but,
in the course of fifteen or twenty years, as the trade
continues to grow, this property rises again in value,
being occupied for manufacturing purposes or for sale-
rooms, and so recoups in large measure, if not fully, all
past losses.

But citizens of our " no mean city " have grounds
for rejoicing in its prosperity not simply as regards its
commercial importance, but also in its moral, intellectual, and legal aspects.   There is no need to dwell
upon the many philanthropic and kindly influences at
work in our midst.   The support given to hospitals, to
children's homes and refuges, and to home and foreign
missions, tells of many who are striving each to fill the
niche prepared for him in the scheme of the world's
uplifting.

The movement for the education of the people has

taken a deep hold of the sympathies of our citizens, and our city has assumed a status in the educational world second only to London and the ever-famous centres, Oxford and Cambridge. Our own university and colleges, schools of the higher grade for men and women, together with our public and board schools, are producing a change within all classes of society, which will have a marked influence in all the varied relations of our people. We have taken rank amongst the largest cities in the empire as a publishing centre, being exceeded in this particular only by Edinburgh and London.

In medicine we stand high, and in the musical world only London outshines us.

Our activity in legal matters will be touched upon in a later chapter.

With reference to municipal administration, it needs but little argument to enforce the truth of the statement that economy is easier in a larger than in a smaller town. With the administrative ability that a large corporation like Greater Manchester would furnish, supplying gas, water, and public baths, and maintaining streets, sewage, and police, under the management of the various committees, saving would be effected and advantages enjoyed which the writer believes it impossible for minor local authorities to secure. To those who are familiar with the management of large concerns, it will be well known that a manager with twenty assistants under him can by virtue of his developed capacity and extended experience as easily direct forty as twenty men; so, too, in the

D

collection of accounts, in the purchase of land, the laying out of a new district in the neighbourhood of new railways or a ship canal, and in a thousand and one ways, concentrated action would be both more economical and more effective. The writer has for a long time been an advocate of the amalgamation into one municipality of the whole district and population within a four-mile radius from the Manchester Royal Exchange. All the people within that radius practically depend upon the business earnings of the city, and this is especially the case in the borough of Salford and the district of Moss Side, the two places which resolutely refuse to join Manchester on grounds of economy.

MOSS SIDE OPPOSITION TO AMALGAMATION.

One of their reasons for not joining Manchester is, that the Moss Side district rate is one shilling and eightpence, whilst that of the city of Manchester is three shillings and sixpence. Now, if there were any generosity at all amongst the opponents of amalgamation, they would admit that the one shilling and eightpence does not include the police rate or the charge of criminal prosecutions, which form a considerable item in the Manchester rate. They forget to mention also that Manchester spends £40,000 a year on libraries, art galleries, and other institutions, which the Moss Side people enjoy in common with the citizens of Manchester. And, supposing the landlords are called upon to pay a little higher rate, it has been proven

again and again, as a Scotchman would say, that the
saving that would be effected in gas and water would
more than compensate for any extra rate. If every
landlord would look beyond the immediate present,
and think of the future interests of the great city of
which Moss Side at present practically forms a part,
they would see that the intelligence, the force of facts,
and the necessities of the immediate future are on the
side of the supporters of incorporation, and that at no
distant date those who are now opposed to it would
admit that a wise thing had been done. Are not the
houses of the Moss Side inhabitants illuminated by
their gas,—their baths and closets supplied by the
city's water? Many of their children are educated in
the Manchester schools, their literature is drawn from
the Manchester libraries, their young people bathe in
their magnificent baths, their little ones and they
themselves enjoy a park which is fit for a royal family,
and has been provided without expense to Moss Side.
Remembering all this, they cry out against the city
councillors, and call upon us to look at the expense
incurred in building the magnificent town hall, which
is the envy of all Britain, one had almost said of the
world. Then the Victoria Hotel is brought into the
discussion, as if all the self-denial and good work
the city council had done were lost upon the minds of
these gentlemen, when they thought of the loss to the
city of £50,000 or £60,000. One would not deny the
Corporation of Manchester has made mistakes, but on
the whole the Corporation is one of which Lancashire
and the country generally may be proud. As to the

death rate of Manchester, which was thirty-six in 1868, it was twenty-five in 1888, and why is it not still lower? Simply because most of the best people have gone to live outside, leaving the very poor and destitute and depraved in the city proper. Yet the board school, the ragged schools, and the philanthropic work conducted by many good men and women will, one must believe, so tell upon the habits of the people that Manchester will soon be worthy of as high a character in respect of mortality as it has in so many other matters. If, in addition, there were added the population of Moss Side and other out-townships with their healthy peoples, the city would rise to a higher level commercially, socially, and morally.

AMALGAMATION WITH THE ROYAL BOROUGH OF SALFORD.

So natural is the proposed union with Salford that we are never dissociated by outsiders. We all hail from Manchester. A further proof of the real identity of the communities of Manchester and Salford, along with Moss Side and other districts within the four-mile radius, exists in the fact of so many important public institutions being situated in Manchester, which, nevertheless, in many senses, belong to the entire population. The important colleges, the Mechanics' Institute, the Athenæum, the Warehousemen and Clerks' Provident Society, the principal clubs, the leading banks, the Free Trade Hall, St. James's Hall, the more commodious hotels and restaurants are all in Manchester.

But it is patent that the continued close co-existence of the two leading communities accounts in considerable measure for the existence and strength of these institutions.

In the same way, it is the Manchester Royal Exchange, the Manchester Corn Exchange, the Manchester Waste and also Provisions Exchanges; it is Manchester that has her Chamber of Commerce, her Trade Protection Society, her Home Trade Society. The gain to Salford from amalgamation would be direct and at once; the effect being to give her " her due share and control " in all public institutions and public interests, and to enable her to " reap the full advantage of the situation." The full effect of amalgamation cannot be stated in a money form as a mere question of economy; though here, on the grounds already stated, the writer believes there would be a great saving, an immediate pecuniary gain to Salford, and a sure future gain to the united community.

Great social and civic advantages would be the immediate result of belonging to a city which, whether considered commercially or in its ability to conduct educational and philanthropic labours or to initiate social reforms, might claim to rank as the second city in the United Kingdom. The opinion of foreign customers and of those well acquainted with the feeling of buyers in the British markets is that the question of population carries with it an immense amount of influence, and of that kind likely to be highly beneficial to the trading community. The political effect of the union would be that we should be represented by ten members in the House of Commons. It is to be gathered from the utterances of both Liberal and Conservative speakers that numbers must more and more rule.

The amalgamation within a four-mile radius would give us nearly one-third part of the population of Lancashire, a county containing one-tenth part of the population of England, and, therefore, an important share of influence and power in the council of the nation.

Regarded from whatever standpoint, the best interests of the people, both in the city and the borough, would be served by amalgamation, and it is the writer's firm conviction that both will suffer by continuing to be separate communities. The writer was not born a Mancunian, but "with a great price" purchased his citizenship, having spent more than forty years in commercial labours in the city. It will continue to be his pride and pleasure by any and by all means at his command to enhance the city's interests, uplift her people, and increase her influence as a factor in the life and commerce of the richest and strongest county of the greatest country in the world.

AMALGAMATION.

SALFORD'S NARROW AND SHORT-SIGHTED VIEWS.

The amalgamation of the corporations of Manchester and Salford—in other words, the placing of the two towns under one municipal administration—has not received the approval of the committee to which the Salford council referred the report of the Amalgamation Association of Manchester and Salford. The decision has taken nobody by surprise.

The amalgamation movement has at no time found favour with some of the members of the Salford Town Council, and it has throughout been evident that, unless the ratepayers took up the subject, nothing effective would be accomplished. Some persons were sanguine enough to think that the approval of amalgamation by seventy-two of the principal inhabitants and ratepayers of Salford, and by many others, would be enough to gain for the subject at least an unprejudiced and impartial hearing. But they overlooked the individual feeling against amalgamation which had strikingly manifested itself amongst members of the Salford council. It is well here to recall the passage in the report of the joint committee of Manchester and Salford, which stated that they had not considered the "effect of amalgamation upon the present members of the two corporations, but felt confident that these gentlemen would be animated solely with a regard to the public interests in determining the constitution of the united corporation." It is very doubtful if this expectation has, in Salford, been justified by results.

The opposition of officials to changes which may affect them personally is natural, and it is as great folly to condemn this sort of opposition as it is to be guided by it. There is no ground for the officials of either Manchester or Salford thinking that they would suffer hardship from amalgamation. The joint committee which recommended it said, "With regard to the officials of the two corporations, your joint committee unanimously recommend that the present staffs be transferred to the united corporation, or compensated in accordance with usage in such cases." Nevertheless it is alleged that in Salford there has been active official opposition to amalgamation, and official opposition is not easily resisted by those within its immediate influence. But whatever may be its strength in Salford, it is quite certain that it does not account for rudimentary personal dislike in the council to amalgamation. A dread undoubtedly exists that if Salford is amalgamated with Manchester, the importance and power of Salford councillors and aldermen would be diminished, and in many instances cease to be visible. The dread of somebody being wiped out has prevented many a local combination or arrangement for benefiting the people. This feeling often prevents men, wishful of doing what is right and best, from seeing what is right and best. Publicity and discussion alone can clear away this feeling. The obvious course is not to mask the feeling, but to strike at it until it is diminished or extinguished. When it is out of the way, there will be a chance for amalgamation being considered by the Salford council on its public merits and demerits. It may be that the Salford council is not dominated by this feeling as is imagined. Whether it is or not cannot be accurately known until the close of the present discussion in the council. It will be a good sign if the discussion and its result show that the minority not affected by this personal feeling is larger than supposed. But if it is not, time and discussion will bring about a change, especially if the ratepayers understand the question and assert their opinions and feelings. The report of the Salford committee, after all, only opens, and is very far from ending, the movement towards amalgamation.

The report of the Salford council committee is a polemic, and not a dispassionate statement upon an important civic question. As a display of dialectics it manifests considerable ability, but the employment of the methods used in it will probably render it valueless for good or for mischief. It was perhaps owing to this conviction that the supporters of the report refused on Wednesday to allow its opponents time to prepare their answer. The compilation of the report had occupied nearly five months, yet those who do not agree with it were expected to have their answer ready in as many days. A discussion under these circumstances can neither satisfy the ratepayers of Salford nor strengthen the position of those who are opposed to amalgamation. It betrays an anxiety to get rid of the question without full and competent discussion, which no public body would attempt unless other feelings than a desire for a just conclusion influenced some of its members. Indeed, the course taken shows that the prejudice against amalgamation is stronger than the disposition to arrive at a calm conclusion upon the merits and demerits of the subject. But the speeches which were made on Wednesday, though made under a disadvantage, showed that the report is not as invincible as its authors wish it to be thought. There was enough said to indicate that its figures and inferences are not only assailable, but liable to very grave reflection. This ought even now to have an influence upon the opinion of the council, and to cause it to pause before determining hurriedly a subject which cannot permanently be put aside by fallacies or prejudices. A delay of a month or two can do the Salford council no injury, and it can do the friends of amalgamation no good if their cause is as baseless and as frivolous as it is represented to be in the report of the committee of the Salford council.

The report of the council's committee is merely a controversial reply to the report of the joint committee composed of Manchester and Salford men who considered amalgamation desirable. Of course the council committee could not ignore the arguments and facts in the report of the joint committee. The latter on their side could not advocate amalgamation without putting forward some of the grounds for it. All arguments, however, can have some sort of an answer made to them. The best schemes ever proposed have found it impossible to disarm opposition. A greater part of the arguments in the joint committee's amalgamation report were subsidiary to the main issue. The subsidiary considerations and arguments were intended principally to remove difficulties and not to take the place of the main issue. The Salford council has discussed the subsidiary questions as if they were the main ones, and dwelt only slightly upon the chief question. And what is of more serious import, they have done so from a selfish standpoint. For instance, they practically say we don't want to have anything to do with the magnificent waterworks system of Manchester, so long as we can get our water from it at a lower rate than the Manchester householders and partly at their cost. This is the language and argument of a huckster, and comes ill from the lips of a civic authority directing the affairs of a great community. All the subsidiary arguments of the joint committee may be subject to modification without the main issue being affected. Indeed, if the differences between Manchester and Salford in the question of rates, water, and other matters were not as they appeared to the joint committee from the statements accessible to them, that would not be an argument against amalgamation. These considerations might affect the terms of amalgamation, but not the main issue as to the advisability of amalgamation. The ground on which amalgamation is sought is that the people of Manchester and Salford are one community, and as one community they ought to have one corporation. It means that one community with common interests should not be weakened by being divided. That the whole of the community should act in unity for all that concerns its welfare. That it should combine the whole of its forces to secure the most benefit for its members individually and collectively. That a single community should not be divided, so that it may risk at any time its parts becoming hostile through temporary adventitious circumstances. That its resources should be applied in securing for the whole community all that is possible, and not be divided in a way which incurs the maximum of expenditure and the minimum of efficiency. Is it not a glaring truth, known to every man who is acquainted with the histories of Manchester and Salford, that the consequence in the past of each town having separate local governments has been that money has been wasted which might have been saved, and that works have been carried out in one borough long before they were secured for the other? Manchester men do not support amalgamation merely for their own advantage, and would agree to it on terms which would do away with any such notion. They want to break down the barriers to common action, to common institutions, to united development, and to the union of resources. They want one community working for the expansion of industry and commerce and promoting social progress. This is a noble aim. What has Salford to answer? Nothing but that this is mere sentiment!

The whole of the Salford council committee's argument proceeds on the assumption that the people of Salford is a rival community to that of Manchester, and that, as such, it should get as much as it can at the expense of Manchester. The joint committee referred in their report to the prospective changes which the Ship Canal is expected to make as a reason for the whole community becoming indivisible, so that its compact population may face and encounter unitedly what is necessary in its commercial and industrial interests. The Salford committee takes this as an indication that the canal will give to Salford solid and enduring advantages which it should keep for itself, and on this rests an argument against amalgamation. Perhaps so, but how much more would be the advantage of the canal to Salford if Manchester devoted its powers to develop the Salford side as much as the Manchester side. Then, as to the waterworks. When the Thirlmere scheme is completed, Manchester will have an unlimited supply of good water, none better in the country. The Salford committee urges that Salford did not oppose the Thirlmere scheme because she had nothing to lose but much to gain by it. Manchester arranged in 1847, upon Salford relinquishing a scheme for an independent water supply, to give her up to a million and a half gallons daily at 2·85d. per thousand gallons, and an additional half million of gallons at threepence per thousand gallons. Broughton and Pendleton, which are now incorporated with Salford, do not share in this bargain, but are supplied direct by Manchester. Can anything show more clearly the disadvantage of the two towns having been governed separately? Will this selfish principle help Salford in the future? If her population and industries increase, as they should, and as the corporation contemplate, what about a further supply of water? Manchester is not bound to give Salford more than the two millions of gallons. Will Salford pride herself on her pound of flesh argument when there is a water famine in her midst, through the increasing number of houses and workshops, and will Manchester fail to remember what is now said and the rival attitude assumed ? This water question may be worth consideration in the terms of amalgamation, but ought not to be an objection pure and simple to amalgamation. If the Salford council think the Salford district should have, on joining Manchester, some compensation for this two millions of gallons of water, why does it not say so ? The Salford council has one kind of consideration for the Salford district, and another for Broughton and Pendleton. It leaves Broughton and Pendleton to the Manchester corporation, and gives them no benefit from its cheap water supply. Salford makes on the water from Manchester a profit of upwards of six thousand pounds a year, which goes to benefit the rate-payers in the Salford district, whilst Manchester is not allowed to make any profit on its waterworks. Neither Broughton nor Pendleton receive a penny from the profits of water, but have to pay for water what Manchester charges. Space will not at present allow of our going further into this argument, but we have said sufficient to show the spirit in which the whole question has been treated by the Salford council report.

The question of rates is a complicated one, but the figures given in the Salford council committee's report, from which we may hereafter show reason for dissenting, show an advantage to Salford over Manchester of only one penny farthing in the pound, or a sum of £3,372 per annum. If this is the measure now of the pecuniary loss that Salford would sustain by amalgamation, surely it might be set against the £6,000 that Salford makes out of Manchester water, and which advantage the district might continue to have if the people in it cannot rise above this paltry selfishness to secure the incontestably greater advantages from amalgamation. The whole financial argument of the Salford committee rests on the assumption that the expenditure of Manchester is going to increase immensely whilst her assessments increase slowly, but that Salford is going to spend nothing whilst her assessments are increasing rapidly. Is it reasonable—is it common-sense—to suppose that Salford can increase its population at the rate of twenty to thirty per cent every ten years without an enormously increasing expenditure to provide for the health and comfort of the people? An united corporation would quickly discover that as much money proportionate to population needs to be spent in Salford as in Manchester. Nay, if Salford is to be developed according to its needs, if it is to be made equal with

Manchester in all that the latter enjoys, if the other side of the Irwell is to cease to be distinguished as a different world in commercial, residential, and other aspects, if Salford is to be remodelled as Manchester must be, according to our better sanitary knowledge, then heaps of money will have to be spent upon it. It is useless to suppose that under amalgamation Manchester will need much and Salford little. Both can have what they need more economically and better if united than if separate. The fallacy underlying the Salford argument is the assumption that the expenditure of the "royal borough" will decrease, and have no extra demands, though in wealth and population it grows at an amazing pace.—*Manchester City News.*

CHAPTER II.

MANCHESTER HOME-TRADE HOUSES.

THERE has been much discussion and correspondence of late as to the wholesale home-
trader's prospects in Manchester. "An exodus of
merchant houses, such as was never seen before,"
characterises the last few years in the opinion of
"Manchester Man," writing to the *Drapers' Record.*
He says, the effect of a walk round the Infirmary is
saddening; "To let," or "This warehouse will be
divided to suit tenants," meets the eye at every turn.
Another says, what is again and again being reported,
that "the old houses have ceased to exist, and the
trade is being absorbed by others." And, again, "the
merchant must cease and only the manufacturer remain; all the old landmarks of the town will be
removed." The same facts are referred to in an able
letter to the *Manchester City News* of November 3rd,
1888. The correspondent says: "During late years an
undue proportion of the wholesale home-trade houses,
old and young firms, have gone out of business or come
to grief, and of those existing now, a few only have increased their trade considerably. . . . The change
has been more of an epidemic character than one of
isolated cases of disease. It has carried off old and
young alike." In three articles in the *City News*, of

dates November 24th, December 1st, and December 8th, 1888, the same facts are re-stated: "That Manchester is rapidly losing her supremacy as a distributing centre will hardly be denied. The purchasing power of the people has increased largely during the past thirty years, but our home trade has certainly not increased in the same ratio. On the contrary, appearances indicate retrogression. Drapers from outlying districts do not come to Manchester in the numbers or with the frequency of former days. The fancy trade is gravitating to London, and, unfortunately for us, the heavy trade appears likely to follow. The provincial wholesale houses, who now go, as far as possible, direct to manufacturers, are becoming more formidable competitors, and are yearly securing a larger share of the trade."

Now, to the writer the aspect of business matters is decidedly more cheerful, and our home trade offers a vastly better prospect for rising and industrious young men in the future, than some of the extracts quoted imply. When the writer was a young man he, too, was accustomed to see the old and honoured names in Cannon Street, High Street, Church Street, Fountain Street, Piccadilly, and latterly in Dale Street, Portland Street, Parker Street, York Street, and Mosley Street; to many of which reference was made in the last chapter.. These localities are to-day largely occupied by what are known as the home-trade houses, firms which at the present time have little or no connection with the foreign or colonial trade. General shipping houses are spread all over the district within three-quarters of a mile from the Infirmary; but there is no need in the present connection to make any particular reference to the shipping houses as such, except to say that they have immensely increased during the past twenty years, alike in number, importance, and repu-tation, and now cover with their palatial buildings the most important parts of our city, and employ directly and indirectly a very large portion of the population in and around the town.

Returning to the home-trade houses, reference has been made to the decay and removal of old and respected firms. It would be as well, instead of dwelling upon these changes, to look at the number of rising firms that are to be found in the fancy trade, the ready-made clothes, boots and shoes, and the mantle trade, many of whom bid fair to rival, in the extent of business and wealth, if not to excel, the magnates of the past. In the list of new concerns, mention should be made of the great co-operative institution in Balloon Street, Manchester. The writer ventures to say that the turnover in the houses now existing will be found to exceed by some millions of pounds sterling the returns made by the firms in the good old times; and if the men of the present day were as unostentatious, as atten-tive, and as industrious as the men of the past genera-tion, there would be a still larger and more satisfactory business done. Referring to a letter of the present writer in the same issue, a leader in the *City News* of October 27th, 1888, says: "Our correspondent is right when he says that substantial reasons can be given for the disappearance of most old concerns. It is a mistake to imagine that old firms disappear from no fault of their own. Failure in either an old or new concern is due in both alike to inherent weakness. Nobody supposes that old concerns are thrown into the shade or compelled to retire when they have the same capital, business capacity, and energy as their new rivals. Surely, if the latter can hold their own, the former, with their old connection, should be able to do so likewise. In business, as in everything else, it is the fittest which survives. Unless old concerns adapt themselves to their continually changing environment, it is impossible for them to survive. And why should they? Why should old firms be maintained by props of prejudice, custom, or sentimental sympathies? These supports will never be of much use for any length of time to a house struggling with a host of competitors. Those firms prosper most which serve their customers best. If a house will not spend money wisely in developing its business, then its trade will go to other concerns which comply with this requirement. If it refuses to deal liberally with its customers, its customers will go where they are dealt with liberally. If the partners in a concern are too big to welcome their customers, the latter will find a welcome elsewhere. If principals do not take an active part in superintending the various departments of their business, nor in encouraging the enterprise and energy of those under them, they will soon find themselves below those who do. If capital is withdrawn by old partners and not replaced by new ones, it is unwise to carry on business in the same extensive way; and, if it is attempted to do so, success is not possible. If we regret the ill success of some old firms, should we not rejoice at the progress of others and at the growth of new ones? Why should not the new men have our sympathy in their struggle, and our admiration at their success? Business cannot stand still. It must either go backwards or forwards. The fact that all the rewards of business are not confined to a set of old concerns is a stimulus to the energy of every new comer. The progress of many concerns testifies that if people adapt themselves to the wants of the day, and pursue their avocations with intelligence and energy, there is yet room for prosperity."

It must be borne in mind that the textile and kindred trades are very varied in their character, and employ the highest talent we can find amongst designers, artists, and manufacturers. It is difficult, nay it is impossible, for any one to measure the possibilities in the different branches of these businesses, between the plain article which satisfies the tastes and desires of the West Indian coolie or the natives of Iceland, to the beautiful and artistic article of dress which would suit the taste of the young ladies of our city. There is room to employ a diversity of talent in the workshop, the mill, and the Manchester warehouse, which latter is the saleroom for their various products. The writer ventures to say that the skill and capacity of individuals engaged in producing goods for the home-trade houses have yet ample space for development, and that, instead of there being fewer warehouses wanted, there should be more.

E

Take, for instance, the fancy business as understood in the home trade. This has not by any means secured the high position which the population of the north of England warrants. Then, the ready-made trade, the boot and shoe trade, though there are some enterprising firms in these branches in the city, no one will say they fully meet the buying powers of the business men who visit this market. They also can be still further and largely developed. The same remarks apply to the mantle trade, a business which requires great skill and ingenuity, and which is yet in its infancy. Then, the carpet and furnishing business. This is a large and ever-increasing branch, but is neglected in this city.

The writer would call the attention of manufacturers to the want of more novel and beautiful designs in counterpanes and quilts. In eider-downs the development has been wonderful, and met with the success which the artistic taste displayed has well merited. Strange, while all other goods used in domestic furnishing have been improving in design, style, and utility, quilts have not received the attention which an article of such large consumption demands, and which it would pay to bestow. We hear from the Black Country of great progress in the products of the sheet-iron makers; that they are able to make sheets so fine and pure, and capable of being folded, that addresses presented to Mr. Gladstone were written upon them. Is there any genius amongst the sheet and quilt manufacturers of this manufacturing district who can strike out a new idea, and develop this vast industry, bringing beauty and attractiveness of design into an article of such constant and all-round service?

Notwithstanding the possibilities of further progress and development in different branches, any person who will count up the comparatively new but successful firms, which are to be found in the locality occupied by home-trade houses, will find cause for rejoicing rather than sadness. The extreme, and one might say interesting, variety of goods, which are sold in our various warehouses, will employ a great diversity of skilled labour, and capable men as masters and servants. It is not possible for any half dozen firms to meet the wants of traders and their customers, the millions who populate England and her colonies.

Let us dwell for a moment upon the variety of goods which are sold to-day in home-trade warehouses. Formerly, any of us wanting a coat or a suit of clothes went to the woollen draper and bought the needed quantity of cloth, then took it to the tailor to be made up. If we or our wives and children wanted a pair of boots, we went to get measured at the shoemaker's. If we wanted a bag, a purse, or fancy article, they had to be sought away altogether from the draper, and still more, if an article of furniture was required for our home, the cabinet-maker must be visited. All this is altered. Stocks of all these goods can now be found on the premises of our large drapers, and yet we find most of the large wholesale houses in the city jogging along on the old lines. Why do they not follow the changed habits and conditions of modern life, and provide, so far as their means will allow, what is required by their clients? If any one asks, "Where will you draw the line?" the writer would reply, In dry goods. Any articles—excepting, of course, such bulky articles as coals—which can be required by man, woman, or child, from birth to death, for their persons or their homes, should be supplied, but not soft goods, that is, provisions. We may rest assured that there will always be a large number of merchants required to conduct so large and varied a business. The centres of textile manufacturing industry, which *must* be visited by the wholesale buyers of our warehouses, exist in various parts of our own country, in Scotland, Ireland, and Wales, and also in Germany, France, Italy, Switzerland, Austria, and Russia. The goods selected from all these centres, together with the article of our own manufacture, are distributed from Manchester over the whole of Britain, our colonies, and to the continents of Europe and America, we might say the world. The great and almost immeasurable diversity of taste and culture, and the corresponding variety of requirements to be found within so wide an area of distribution, will necessitate a large number of distributors, who possess capital and ability—men and women who carefully study the wants of their clients, and who can stock their warehouses with suitable materials for meeting their demands. It is absurd to say, as some do, that the trade will be swallowed by a few houses. Of course, the best-managed houses, and the most capable and industrious men who have capital, will rise above others, and secure a larger trade. But that three or six men or firms in Manchester do or ever can possess all the genius and force necessary to absorb and conduct the whole of the textile branch, and satisfy the tastes of the thirty thousand to fifty thousand merchants and drapers, who deal with Manchester houses, is beyond any intelligent man's belief. Take, for instance, mantles, ready-mades, furniture, prints, haberdashery, fancy goods, dress goods, or almost any branch: a moment's reflection will show that there is both room and need for a large number of merchants and general dealers, persons or firms, who devote themselves to one, two, or three special articles, apart altogether from the manufacturers. There are at present forty thousand commercial travellers. Now, suppose that, instead of these travellers working from given distributing centres, the whole of the manufacturers in Leicester, Nottingham, Derby, Northampton, Loughborough, Hinckley, Belper, Luton, London, Bolton, Bury, Wigan, Preston, Colne, Clitheroe, Blackburn, Haslingden, Bacup, Accrington, Heywood, Rochdale, Hebden Bridge, Halifax, Bradford, Dewsbury, Batley, Huddersfield, Leeds, Wakefield, Barnsley, Heckmondwike, Sowerby Bridge, Todmorden, Stockport, Ashton, Denton, and a score of other towns in this country, where textile goods are made, together with towns in Scotland, Ireland, and Wales, as well as in the numerous continental centres of textile manufacture,—let us suppose that all these were to send their own travellers to the drapers in the cities and towns of this, not to say of other countries, the loss of time and the annoyance to the retail trader would only be exceeded in foolish impracticability by the wasteful expenditure that would be incurred, and for which the people, the real consumers, must pay.

The reader will thus see the necessity there is for wholesale warehouses and fixed centres for distribution. They must exist; and for economy of expenses the fewer general centres the better. The writer, for one, believes there are men possessing the requisite talent, if they had the confidence, to establish new departments and new firms or companies, and that the enlargement which has taken place within the past few years is but the beginning of greater and better things for Manchester. Men who begin now will be free from the demoralising influence attending the prosperity of 1862 and 1870 to 1874, which stifled the energy and almost destroyed the ability that had up to that date made Manchester merchants and manufacturers the best-known and respected men in the country. The high prices which ruled during the American war, followed as it was so quickly by the Franco-German war, started traders in habits of living, lifted them and many of their men into spheres or positions, from which it is hard to descend. Many date their trade troubles from those periods. Long may it be before such a time of commercial demoralisation is experienced again.

There can be no doubt that all the suffering referred to by other writers has been greatly aggravated and intensified by the great depression in our agricultural districts. This, however, seems now to be giving place to better times. Our farmers are more hopeful and buoyant, and certainly many branches of industry throughout the midland and northern counties are improving. There is more hope and confidence, and better profits all round are to be expected.

Further, if the outlook from the present aspect of business matters were as dark as some would picture it, what is the answer to the question of fact that several of the largest concerns have so greatly increased their business and the size of their premises? They are labouring in the same neighbourhood, breathe the same atmosphere, buy in the same markets, and they are not sons of that man of great stature, named in the Book of Chronicles, whose fingers and toes were four-and-twenty—six on each hand and six on each foot. "No one," says the writer of the leader in the *City News*, already quoted, "surely will venture on the bold statement that new concerns prosper by reason of adopting improper business methods. If improper business practices injure the old concerns, how can it be imagined that the same practices will not injure the new concerns? Is it not to be feared that new departures which men make in business, because of their foreseeing likely changes amongst customers, are often described without reason as unsound or unfair methods? Many of them are nothing of the kind, and this is seen by the fact that departures at first denounced become in a short time very general, and at last the prevailing custom. If the men who were once the chief warehousemen in Manchester were to look to-day into some of the large Manchester warehouses, they would be simply bewildered at the enormous number of articles dealt in, many of which were, in their day, foreign to their business; some did not even exist. It is more than probable that those gentlemen would not hold the position they once had in business if they lived now and adhered to their old principles and modes of working. . . . During the past twenty years, coincidently with the change that has been taking place in the wholesale and retail drapery houses at home, hundreds of thousands of our countrymen—English, Irish, Scotch, and Welsh—have gone out to the different countries abroad. They have taken British notions, British industry, and business capacity with them to the East and West Indies, to America, Canada, Scandinavia, to Africa, South America, and some parts of China. They are trading on much the same lines that are being followed in this country; many of them come over to England to buy their wares just as regularly and even more frequently than our customers from remote parts of our own land. And yet, with a few notable exceptions, amongst the home-trade houses they fail to find the goods required for their various markets, notwithstanding that Manchester is the centre of our various industries. It is notorious that the colonial trade is the backbone of the Glasgow home-trade houses. Taken all round, the colonial business is the most rapidly increasing and prosperous that England possesses, and the goods used are the reflex of what are sold in the home trade. There was, therefore, no reason why Manchester, had she exerted herself, might not have had a larger share of this trade."

Assuredly, commercial wisdom does not reside in

apathy, or in holding aloof from the demands which the altered conditions of trading impose. The fact of "a modern drapery establishment bearing a greater resemblance to an American dry goods store than to an old English shop" should in itself decide the course for the wholesale trader to adopt. The house that suits itself to the draper's requirements will naturally secure his custom. Why should not this be true of the Manchester wholesale houses? Situated in the very heart of the most important manufacturing district in the world, whose products are in universal demand—and with the extension of civilisation an increasing demand—Manchester is and must be the great centre for distribution. Within a radius of forty miles of the Manchester Exchange we have seven millions of people, and when Salford realises the importance of her amalgamation with Manchester, and the accruing advantages begin to be felt, then, as the centre of this vast population and the second city in the empire, we shall, if the home-trade houses will rise to the position and the opportunity, take our proper place as a trading community. Our facilities for producing, arising from our easy access to coal and iron, the nerve and sinew of manufacture, and for distributing, arising from our central position, should not only encourage the further development of existing firms, but be an incentive to energetic young men who desire to make their mark and to rank amongst the merchants of our city. The modern facilities for travelling enable our buyers to visit any market, at home or abroad, on equal terms with buyers from any other place in the kingdom; and the construction of the Manchester Ship Canal will give us still further advantages in this respect; cotton, wool, and other raw materials will soon be laid almost at our mill doors from the vessels which bring them from all parts of the world.

The importance of the Ship Canal, which is now rapidly approaching completion, to Manchester as a trading centre it would be difficult to exaggerate. The very fact of the passing of the act, " after the most prolonged struggle in the history of private bill legislation," speaks for itself. The commercial evidence before six committees of the two Houses of Parliament was so convincing as to secure the verdict of the most competent men in Westminster in its favour. The importance to the future trade of the country of opening up direct intercourse between the centre of such large manufacturing and mercantile operations and other nations was clearly recognised, and should be recognised by all who are interested in the future of Manchester as a trading centre. The effect of the inland water-carriage will be to facilitate and cheapen the moving of raw materials—cotton, corn, timber, wool, fur, &c., which, being bulky, have seriously suffered from the burden of the railway charges. Great loss of time in transhipping and extra expense result from unloading in Liverpool goods for the greater part of which Manchester is the natural centre of distribution. The continuation of the ocean voyage of a vessel a few hours' steam inland is so inappreciable in relation to the whole distance traversed, that vessels would only require the same freight to Manchester as required to Liverpool. An illustration is given by the parallel case of Havre, at the mouth of the Seine, and Rouen, sixty miles on that river above Havre, the freights of ocean-going vessels to either port being equal. This clearly does away with the whole cost of the railway carriage between Liverpool and Manchester. Owing to this important fact, the maximum tariff fixed by the Manchester Ship Canal Act, 1885, which the company may charge, is fixed at exactly one-half of the combined port and railway charges as they stood at the time the Act was obtained, in other words a reduction of fifty per cent. With these increased facilities trade will naturally expand; the volume of traffic will be greater; and the railways, and even Liverpool itself, will be not injured, but benefited. There is no doubt that we have suffered severely from the effects of the high rates of transit, both import and export. For years past everything has been done to reduce the cost of production; the energies of the proprietors of our various manufactories have been devoted to this end in the speeding and development of machine power, the reduction of wages, and of general standing expenses. Every decrease in the cost of production to the manufacturer means, in the long run, increased ability for the trader buying from him to compete in home or foreign markets. When the canal is in active operation, we shall be materially helped in our efforts to contend with strong competitors in foreign markets by the minimising of the charges for carriage to the sea. There is every probability, too, that ships, which now load exclusively in London, will come up to

Manchester, part loaded, to complete their cargoes, in the same way that ships now load partially in Glasgow and fill up at Liverpool. This will again effect a very large saving, which will tell in favour both of manufacturers and merchants in the race of competition.

Moreover, what is to prevent a large business coming through the port of Manchester from Huddersfield, Batley, Dewsbury, Leeds, Sheffield, the Potteries, and Birmingham district, and from the coalfields of Lancashire, South Yorkshire, and North Staffordshire? In that case not only would Manchester be benefited, but the industries of these districts would be largely developed. The establishment of works along the banks of the new canal cannot fail to add to our prosperity. It was the prospect of this new field of labour for the increasing population that largely helped to secure the sympathy and gain the strong and hearty approbation of the industrial classes of this city and district. It was the deep immovable conviction that the sons and daughters of the present generation would have a future in their own country, and not the outlook of a miserable pittance here or life on a foreign and unknown shore, that led fifty thousand men to assemble on common ground on Saturday, June 21st, 1884, to say, so far as their means and strength could say, that the canal should be made. The writer will not forget a working man coming up to him after one of the many meetings he attended in support of the scheme, who addressed him by name, and said, " God bless you, and all the other gentlemen that are working so hard in this great scheme ! It will do us all good, and our children, too."

It was but the voice of thousands, who thought and felt as he did, but did not express it in the same homely way.

It may be interesting here to refer to a passage in Baines' work on *Lancashire and Cheshire*, already quoted, bearing upon the question, which, it will be seen, was mooted so early as the year 1697, of navigation to Manchester.

About the year 1694 the river between Runcorn and Warrington was improved, chiefly by the exertions of Mr. Patten. We have no information as to the nature of the works that were constructed in that part of the river, but it is probable that they consisted chiefly of buoys and lights. But they were found to be so useful that about one-half of the whole quantity of goods forwarded from Liverpool to the interior, and from the interior to Liverpool, was from that time sent by river up to Warrington, instead of by land carriage, so early as the year 1697. The effect was to add very greatly to the trade both of the port of Liverpool and of the inland districts of Lancashire, and also greatly to strengthen the general wish that the rivers Mersey and Irwell should be rendered navigable from Warrington to Manchester. Mr. Patten, writing to Richard Norris, Esq., M.P. for Liverpool, in January, 1697, in support of a bill then before Parliament for removing fish weirs, which destroyed salmon and hindered navigation in navigable rivers, points out the injury which those obstructions produce, and the advantages that would arise from rendering the river Mersey navigable from Warrington to Manchester and Stockport. Writing to Mr. Norris on the 8th January, 1697, he says : " I am informed that there is a design to bring a bill into the House of Commons against fish weirs, that hinder navigation in navigable rivers, and that take and destroy fish, and the fry of fish. You may well know the mischief that is done in the river Mercy [Mersey], or at least have frequently heard what vast numbers of salmon trout are taken, so as to supply all the country and market towns twenty miles round, until the country is cloyed, and when they cannot get sale for them they give them to their swine. Your brother did formerly take three or four salmon a week at a fishing, in or near Speke, but of late hath taken very few or none, of which he hath complained to me, and he imputes this loss to the destruction of the fry, and hath often threatened to prosecute your fisheries." " Then, again," he observes, "these weirs are as mischievous another way, by hindering the passage of ships, boats, and barges; as, for example, in the same river Mersey, what a vast advantage it would be to Liverpool if the river were made navigable to Manchester and Stockport. Since I made it navigable to Warrington, there have been sent to Liverpool and from Liverpool 2,000 tons of goods a year, and I believe as much by land, which, if the river were cleared of weirs, would all go by water; for the river to Manchester is very capable of being made navigable at a very small charge; and this would encourage all tradesmen in Manchester, Stockport, Macclesfield, Congleton, Bolton, Bury, Rochdale, some part of Yorkshire, Derbyshire, to come to Liverpool and buy their goods, instead of going to

Chester, Bristol, or London; the carriage would be so easy and cheap. I think it would nearly double the trade of Liverpool."*

With the immediate prospect on the completion of the canal of saving Lancashire alone £500,000 per annum; with a present business aspect not by any means so gloomy as some would picture it; with the opening up of new industries on and around the canal, is there not every likelihood of improved business in every department? With industries localised around us, a population born and reared under the noise of loom and spindle, inhaling the atmosphere of bleach and dye works, learning from earliest life to manipulate the raw materials, driven not only by the necessities of family life, but also by what might be called an industrial instinct, to an acquaintance with the various processes of manufacturing and finishing goods, so that in mechanism, in experience, and in habits of industry the population of this district is not excelled in this or in any country in the world, we have a right to say that this is and ought to be a grand centre for mercantile operations, and to look forward to our future with hope and confidence.

Returning to the business of the warehouse, so far nothing has been said on the subject of dating forward. It is a vexed question, and a brief statement of opinion, with the reasons for it, is all that would be in place here. As the reader will know, there are many, including the correspondent, "Manchester Man," already

---

* Page 82, vol. ii.

referred to, who trace all the troubles of the home trade to this source. " The merchants here have never recognised the force of the fact that there is a competition of terms as well as of prices, and that the former is often the greater factor of the two." " Town Traveller," in the issue of May 11th, 1889 *(Drapers' Record)*, says, " The dating-forward system is increasing amongst the London houses and that continuously. I venture the opinion that until Manchester and other centres adopt the same system, nearly all buyers, especially those who do their own counting-house work, will favour the London houses." A " South of England Draper," writing in the next issue, May 17th, is of the same opinion: " The 'dating forward' may be a rotten system, I am not arguing on that, but as long as it is a recognised system of the trade, as it now is, and Manchester refuses to recognise it, so long will Manchester have cause to complain of the transition of its trade."

The practice indicated as necessary to the salvation of the Manchester home trade is the giving of two or three months' extra credit on special occasions. The slowness of Manchester wholesale houses to adopt this practice is said to account for the progress other firms are making in competing with them for the draper's custom. Now, long experience and observation have convinced the writer that the drapers are amongst the shrewdest and most capable traders in the country, and the best of them, who have means and are judges of the goods they buy, will not be long in finding out the different values offered by the various houses.

All intelligent men in the wholesale trade know pretty nearly the average profit, and can, therefore, say whether it is paying a house to sell at the ordinary profit, and give other facilities which they cannot afford. Extra dating and discount must be made up in price, and the safest and most reliable men know this and buy accordingly. It would be well for every house to decline dating forward any plain cotton goods, which have to be paid for quickly, and on which there is a very small margin of profit, a fact well known to all buyers. Dating of season goods and an exceptional sale are necessities for which all can make allowance.

The evils of the system, in the view of the writer, can be best illustrated by an example. Suppose a respectable young firm, wholesale, does £120,000 per annum. One extra month's terms means a further credit of £10,000 in their books. This capital cannot be added in the year from profits, and must therefore be borrowed, or the time given must be bought back by an extra discount for cash or bills, or it must be taken from the manufacturer in extended terms under certain conditions; this means at least full one-half per cent loss, or addition to expenses; and this is not all, as we will presently show. Now, the wholesale trade is competed for so keenly that a difference like this takes a very important part of the profit. What is the inevitable result? Naturally, the expenses being increased the price must be raised to recoup the loss. But a trader replies, "Few men can tell to one-half or one per cent." Yes, but this is not all. The merchant finds that a number of unscrupulous

F

traders have started business in various towns. The fact of their taking the extra time is not the whole nor the end of the evil. The trade of the place in which they have commenced business will only support a certain number of dealers, and the effect often is that the old, respectable, reliable customer of many years' standing is so beaten in the race that he fails, and the wholesale house has to accept ten shillings in the pound. Or, if the old trader is too strong and beats his new rival, which frequently happens, then the last comer succumbs; but, instead of receiving ten shillings in the pound, you find his trading has all been on the capital of the creditor. He has little or no capital of his own, and when the winding-up comes under an assignment, it is five shillings, or, if in the court, perhaps three shillings or three shillings and sixpence. Taking in these losses, there is a larger percentage to be added to expenses. The trader would find, by analysing the facts, that he has to pay more than one-half or one per cent for the gratification of his desire for dating forward. It is a pernicious system whichever way one looks at it, and is productive of untold trouble and evil to wholesale and retail traders alike.

OBSERVATIONS MADE AT A SHAREHOLDERS' MEETING.

We will take this opportunity of making a few remarks. You will observe some very important changes in the balance sheet. The first deserving your attention is the very cheering improvement in the amount of the reserve fund. Next you will observe the item of liability to Mrs. Rylands on one side and to mortgagees on the other have both been removed, and in place of them four-per-cent debenture bonds, value £900,000, appear; and these, as we ventured to prophesy, have been issued without any cost to the company, except the necessary legal charges and printing of the documents, an operation few companies could accomplish. We have now in *land, buildings, plant, stocks,* and *debts* a total of £3,829,003. 4s. 8d., against which the outside public have claims amounting to £748,082. 12s. 8d., the balance being your own capital. Our returns for the year 1889 were in excess of those on the year 1888 or of any previous year. Our profits were fair, but not quite equal to our expectations. On this point let me say that there are two facts we must not forget, they must ever be borne in mind, viz., increase in expenses, necessitated by our present mode of doing business, and consequent curtailment of net profits, unless we can concurrently enlarge the turnover.

Our trade during the past half year has been seriously affected by the advance in raw cotton, and our inability to get a corresponding advance in manufactured goods. When you remember the large departments for the sale of these goods, and that to supply them it takes six hundred bales of cotton per week, equal to thirteen million three hundred thousand pounds per annum, you will at once recognise the important effect of any change in the value of the raw material.

On the eve of one of Napoleon's great battles, one

of his people said to him "*Circumstances* are against you." "Sir," he replied, "circumstances I make, or control, I don't bow to them." That was very fine in speech, but he found, as many others have, that he had, on more than one occasion, to bow. The idea is right, not to give way without careful consideration when things around you indicate progress; if we have the spirit and purpose to achieve great things, we often succeed. Napoleon, however, found the snow and cold of the Russian climate more terrible than the Russian army; he found Wellington, at Waterloo, leading the true, indomitable, and never-beaten British soldiers too strong for him. Under both circumstances he had to bow. During the past year the manufacturers of Lancashire found antagonists in various forms they never contemplated, which have been too strong for them; *they* have had to bow, and come off *not* victorious. The net profits of the last year, and especially of the last half, have not been satisfactory to them. Out of eighty-six cotton companies whose figures can be seen, the distribution has only been at the average rate of three and five-eighths per cent; but we are all hopeful that a better state of trade is before us.

RESERVE FUND.

We wish to say a word or two to a few friends who are very anxious about our reserve fund. Some wish us to hold our hands, stop all further additions to it, and distribute whatever profit is made amongst the shareholders in the form of an increased dividend;

others ask that the whole of the fund now existing, and all further additions, should be invested outside the business. Now, as to the first point, you will observe in the balance sheet, land, buildings, plant, &c., £1,047,452. As a going concern, some of our works are worth more than they stand at in the books of the company, and, by our present process, all will be in the same position in a reasonable time. But, gentlemen, our duty as directors, and, we venture to say, your duty as shareholders, is to look at the value, not only as a going concern, but to consider the position the company would be in if we had to wind up. We don't hesitate to say, if that disagreeable day were to arrive soon, the loss we should incur by a forced sale would not be covered by the reserve we now hold; hence our strong desire to still further increase it, until we can feel independent of all contingencies; and by so doing we shall be strengthening and increasing the value both of the shares and the debentures. As to the second point, Why don't we invest the reserve fund outside? Well, suppose we took the £300,000, we could not obtain solid securities carrying interest exceeding three or three and a quarter per cent, which would bring in, say, £9,000 to £10,000 per annum. This movement would compel us to do one of three things—we must either issue the remaining £300,000 of debentures, at a cost of £12,000 per annum; or call up capital on share account at a still higher cost and risk; or, which would be a still greater loss in money, and a much more serious loss of prestige, that is, cease to take our full discount on goods we purchase. Gentlemen, we are not like an insurance company, which has no means of utilising its capital except by making outside invest-ments. We shall not be liable to any anxiety whilst we maintain our present easy financial position of being able to pay cash for all purchases and take full advan-tage of all discounts; we feel confident the course we are adopting is the best and wisest in the interests of the company, and will tend more than any other to maintain the high reputation the company enjoys, and will, at no distant date, enable us safely to enlarge the dividend—a pleasure, we assure you, we are looking forward to quite as earnestly as any member of the company; but being in full knowledge of the whole working of the concern and its responsibilities, and feeling the importance above all other things of safety, not only for the present, but for many years to come, we prefer to pursue the course which so far has com-mended itself to the great body of shareholders, and we believe will do so still.

HOME-TRADE HOUSES.

During the past few weeks, we have been spoken to by gentlemen of this city, by many customers, and by some of our own people about the changes which have taken place in the houses engaged in the home trade, and asked to make some observations or explanations about same. We will endeavour to say a few words on this subject, because we fear, nay, we know, that in some cases the enquiries arise from anxiety as to the future of the Manchester trade. We don't consider it desirable or prudent to go into particulars about any firm or individuals; we prefer rather to state a few facts applicable to our own company, and leave you to draw your own inferences. Don't forget, however, that though a few old concerns have gone out, a number of new ones have commenced and others have been largely developed and will no doubt increase.

In a large concern, like the one in the interests of which we meet to-day, it is of the first importance there should be as leaders men of experience, judgment, and untiring industry, who will carefully consider and decide upon the best courses of action to further its development and maintain its stability. As manufacturers and merchants they must lead and not follow. Hence the importance of their having—

1. All the works in the highest state of efficiency, and attempt no branch of manufacture in which they cannot equal or excel all competitors.

2. They must have careful and prudent men, who not only know the class and value of raw materials required in their various factories and works, but also know the right moment to buy.

3. They require capable and industrious men as managers in the works, who are *practically* acquainted with the department of manufacture they undertake to control, who will exercise energy, and give constant attention in the discharge of their duties.

4. They must have well-appointed and appropriate warehouses, affording proper facilities for exhibiting the goods offered for sale.

5. There must be in the warehouse able and

judicious men as heads of departments, supported and helped by travellers of the highest repute, and salesmen sincerely and earnestly interested in their work, a class of men I am happy to say the directors have around them here.

6. They should have strong, prudent, far-seeing men, whose integrity must be equal to their intelligence as the ruling authorities in their counting-houses and offices, men who know how to judge of character, to utilise the forces around them, to know whom and to what extent they should give credit, who should be acquainted with and capable of managing the finances and official work of a great corporation like this, keeping themselves acquainted with the rates of exchange as well as the commercial and bankruptcy laws of the different countries with which the house is trading.

Given these six separate and necessary conditions, and the company or firm has but one important and serious difficulty to fear, viz., the want of cohesion or true and faithful co-operation of the members of the board or partners in the firm. If there is a lack of personal continuous oversight, or if there be dissension and antagonism amongst the heads of the concern, then the finest, most financially strong, and well-organised concern will fail to hold its ground, it will gradually lose its position. Speaking for the members of your board, I can unhesitatingly say so far there has been hearty and united effort for the general weal; to affirm that they have no differences of judgment would be to state they are not men capable of forming opinions and expressing them. *So far*, whatever differences have arisen have been promptly and happily settled, and there seems no reason at the moment to anticipate any change in their mode of procedure or the lessening of their energies. They are all anxious to improve the business, and, though the extension of terms in the trade and consequent increase of risk, the keen competition and increasing expenses may retard them somewhat, they have the hope and the intention at no very distant date of making what you have a right to expect, an improvement in the rate of dividend. In this, however, as to time and amount, they ask you to favour them with your confidence, remembering that as your reserves increase so does the value of your shares and the solidity of the concern.

CHAPTER III.

RETAIL TRADE IN MANCHESTER GOODS.

RETAIL TRADERS.

THE writer does not believe that any fixed plans and regulations can, of themselves, make a man successful, but if he has intelligence, industry, and tact, combined with a technical knowledge of the various goods he buys, and the necessary capital, then method and rules will help him. He will see for himself the importance of following certain fixed principles.

As to his stock, the character of it must depend upon the town and the district in which he is located. The size or value of his stock will depend largely upon the population he has to work upon. If he is in a large town of more than two hundred thousand people, he needs a less stock in proportion to his turnover than he would in a smaller town; in fact, the result of experience is proof to the writer that from the small place, say of two thousand inhabitants, where the trader has to keep almost everything, to the city of half a million of people, the average stock will vary from twelve weeks' turnover in the larger town to thirty or thirty-six weeks' turnover in the smaller. The following statement may be taken as a guide : In towns of from two thousand to five thousand inhabitants, a draper may hold a stock equal to thirty to thirty-six weeks' turnover; in towns of from five thousand to ten thousand inhabitants, twenty-six to thirty weeks' turnover.

10,000 to	20,000 inhabitants,	24 to 26	weeks' turnover.	
20,000 to	50,000 ,,	20 to 24	,,	,,
50,000 to	100,000 ,,	20 to 22	,,	,,
100,000 to	200,000 ,,	18 to 20	,,	,,
200,000 and upwards ,,		16 to 20	,,	,,

When this population is reached (two hundred thousand and upwards) it greatly depends upon the head of the business as to the amount and character of the stock he keeps. If he decides upon keeping rich and valuable goods, together with carpets and woollens, then the proportion changes.

One matter is of the utmost importance to all small traders. Fresh and clean stock is essential to prosperity. The increased expense of carriage, caused by more frequent purchases, whether at the wholesale house or through the travellers, will be far more than counterbalanced by the smaller stock that is required to be kept, and the quicker payment of accounts that can be made, thereby saving discount. The old habit of buying largely twice a year has quite gone out of fashion; smart, successful drapers are buying or ordering weekly, many daily. The great variety of fancy goods—new things being constantly brought into the market—makes it a necessity to be always ready to take up new productions. This cannot be done if the stock is filled up. The great danger is of buying too much, especially in these times when credit is so cheap and parcels are continually being dated forward. Young tradesmen often get the impression, when they buy on forward date, that the pay day is so far ahead that no disaster can occur; but they find very soon to their cost that dated goods are not only not the cheapest, but that the due date of their bills comes much sooner than they expected. Repeatedly, when being interviewed, young men give their liabilities at, say, £1,200, omitting altogether dated-forward parcels, which, when added, bring up the amount to £1,500 or £1,600. If traders, in addition to the above regulations as to the amount of stock they should hold on an average, would lay down the following golden rule, they would be benefited to an extent they cannot at present comprehend; only experience can sufficiently impress their minds with its importance. Assuming that a trader is doing for the most part a cash trade, he should *never allow his liabilities to trade creditors to exceed two to two and a half times his capital.*

If a tradesman's capital is £500 and he owes £1,250, this gives a total working stock of £1,750. On a stock of this amount he can, according to the size of the town, turn over, say, £3,500, in a large centre £4,000, or in a great population £5,000 per annum.

We will take the moderate-sized town, and say he does £4,000 per annum or about £330 per month; with this turnover he can pay in four months, that is, he can pay within net terms, and have a small margin. Before long economy in the working of his business should place him in a position to take full advantage of discounts, and of special lines and cheap parcels, which are always being placed in the way of a cash man, which but seldom reach the hands of a slow payer.

Where the draper's trade is largely on credit terms, his difficulties are greater; his capital and credit are being put largely into his books, and he has to be content with a smaller stock and a less turnover. His aim must be to restrict, so far as possible, the credit part of his business; buyers will not pay the prices they did formerly to compensate for long credits, and the various organisations for promoting cash business throughout the country are so strong that the shopkeeper must have well-ordered stocks and must sell cheaply. The tendency of legislation for some years past has been to do away with all facilities which foster the credit system, and to force people to do a cash business, and certainly the civil service, co-operative societies, &c., all help to educate the people to this system. If traders generally would more resolutely follow in the same direction great good would be effected, a healthier state of trade would exist, and less anxiety both for the retail and wholesale houses of the country.

In good times, when money is plentiful and people can afford to buy easily and freely, they do not run about so much from one place of business to another to find out the cheapest article; if they see goods they like, they buy them.

As a rule, a draper will be successful if he has a fair, all-round acquaintance with his class of goods, good taste in selection, and the ability to dress his windows attractively—a most important element in the prosperity of any retail concern.

The six points in the draper's charter are:—

1. Capital, consistent with his business requirements.
2. Well-assorted and well-kept stock.
3. Capable and obliging salesmen and assistants.
4. Well-dressed windows.
5. Untiring industry.
6. Economy in every department and good management.

The following paragraphs from the *Colonial Drapers' Journal*, on " Going into Business," are worth quoting:—

Great and ambitious designs are natural to the period of early manhood, when a limited knowledge of the business of life gives confidence and an earnest longing for future success. So the young man looks forward to the time when he will be "master in his own house," with a position in the world. Buoyed by such hopes, he collects his savings and his portion for a start upon the all-important road—the road to fortune. This is the flood-tide to the average young man; for him there appears no other road but that which leads right on to success. He pictures to himself his saving habit and temperate disposition, that he is not afraid of any amount of hard work, and so, filled with economic principles and determinations, he looks round to see what others are doing; seeking information of this friend or that, but, after all, it too often happens that the "pictures of imagination" hide many a harsh fact, leaving hard lessons to be learnt by a trying experience.

Some people there are who, full of sympathy for the young beginner, will point to numerous instances of success with an air of confidence (as though they had been behind the scenes), detailing the wonderful gifts of this man or that, their peculiarities, and extraordinary business capacity; and when asked about the reverse side will be just as ready to attribute this man's want of success to thoughtless extravagance, another's to reckless buying or unsteady habits, &c., and thus reasoning on the most convenient lines, these great advisers will conclude by saying, "You go to work economically and carefully, and you are bound to succeed;" forgetting that " 'Tis not in mortals to command success."

. . . To fit up a shop in a style unsuited to a neighbourhood is to ensure certain failure; fitting and stock adapted to a low-class trade being introduced into a high-class neighbourhood will not attract, while the reverse will have the effect of frightening poor people altogether. Amongst early failures, one of the greatest causes may be included under this head—a young man goes into business from a high-class establishment, where he has been accustomed to "feather bed trade," experience unfitting him for the rough-and-ready system which his limited capital suggests; the whole of his arrangements are made upon the most extravagant scale; both household and shop fittings must be in first-class style; and so the capital is absorbed, for his "white elephants" will not realise when the quiet season comes round. Over-buying is a fearful snare to young men at the present day, although everything should warn them rather to err in the opposite direction. Fashion is entirely opposed to it.

It is always best to calculate the chances of waiting for a trade, and the daily wants which must arise in a new business; for where a man invests his whole capital on the chance of an immense return in six months, disappointment often follows; he finds there are hundreds of things which he has forgotten to buy.

The writer has frequently been asked, when discussing the question of expenses in the management of business, what proportion the rent of premises should bear to the total? Our opinion is that in the drapery trade in large towns, on a business of—

£15 to £25 per week, the rent should not exceed £40 per annum.
£25 to £35   ,,   ,,   ,,   £50   ,,
£35 to £50   ,,   ,,   ,,   £60/70   ,,
£50 to £70   ,,   ,,   ,,   £80/90   ,,
£70 to £100   ,,   ,,   ,,   £100/120   ,,

By the time the returns exceed £100 per week, the character of the business is often changed, and the rules which hold good on the smaller turnover have to be varied according to the altered, enlarged, or changed position of the premises, the character of the business, and according to the widening experience of the proprietor. Rents in smaller towns are less in proportion, but interest on the additional stock it is requisite to keep fully balances this advantage.

CHAPTER IV.

MANCHESTER HOME-TRADE ASSOCIA-TION AND COMMERCIAL TRAVELLERS' ASSOCIATION.

THE writer has been for some years intimately connected with the Home-Trade Association in Manchester. The importance of the matters discussed at its meetings, the energy of its action in critical cases demanding the attention of home traders, and the effective part the association has played in suggesting the introduction or the modification of legal measures affecting trade, entitle its transactions to the notice of all business men. All matters affecting the textile trade are brought forward and discussed; legal questions referring to the trade, *e.g.*, Bankruptcy Law, Married Women's Property Act, Bills of Sale Act, the laws relating to railway traffic, and post-office service, have all from time to time occupied the attention of the committee of the association. The practical experience of the members has in very many cases made its influence felt, and the memorials that have been drawn up and the deputations appointed have been instrumental in correcting some proposed clauses in acts of Parliament, and materially modifying others, to the advantage of trade generally, but especially of the textile traders.

For instance, so.far back as 1870, the association

was in correspondence with the Postmaster-General with regard to a change that had then been recently made in the regulations respecting the transmission of patterns through the post-office; and a memorial was sent up to the Right Honourable the Marquis of Hartington, M.P., the terms of which are as follows:—

To the Right Honourable the Marquis of Hartington, M.P., Her Majesty's Postmaster-General.

THE MEMORIAL OF THE PRESIDENT, VICE-PRESIDENT, AND COMMITTEE OF THE MANCHESTER HOME-TRADE ASSOCIATION,

RESPECTFULLY SHEWETH:

That when your memorialists recently brought under your lordship's consideration a proposal to extend the principle of the book post to articles of all descriptions, and thus to constitute the delivery of small parcels throughout the country a regular branch of the postal service, they ventured to hope that during the recess such proposals would receive your lordship's consideration.

That your memorialists observe with deep regret that the regulations which have since been issued under the ninth section of the Post Office Act, 1870, tend in exactly the opposite direction by declaring that "the pattern and sample post is restricted to *bonâ fide* trade patterns or samples of merchandise," and that "goods sent for sale, or in execution of an order (however small the quantity may be), or any articles sent by one private individual to another, which may not actually be patterns or samples, are not admissible."

That in the opinion of your memorialists this restriction, for which no valid reason exists, will cause great public dissatisfaction, and lead to much difficulty in the administration of the Act.

That as there is practically no limit to the quantity so long as the character of "*bonâ fide* patterns or samples" is maintained on the one hand, nor any definition of what constitutes a "pattern or sample" on the other hand, there is ample opportunity to evade the restriction by so increasing the quantity as to give choice or selection, or the district postmasters must have an arbitrary power to decide what is and what is not a "pattern or sample."

That a case in point has come to the knowledge of your memorialists, where "a *bonâ fide* pattern," consisting of one yard of calico sent by a

G

wholesale house in this city to one of its own travellers, was subjected to a charge of 1s. 8d. for postage, and the post-office authorities state, in reply to a remonstrance, that they intend so to treat everything which could be made an article of sale.

That it is the invariable practice of wholesale houses throughout the country to supply their travellers with "full width" patterns of many of the goods they have to offer for sale, whilst in many cases, particularly in other trades than that represented by your memorialists, a complete specimen of the article itself must be supplied. Any regulation, therefore, which requires that in order to pass through the post-office all articles shall be so cut up or mutilated as to deprive them of their saleable character will vexatiously restrict the use of the pattern post, and, your memorialists submit, will contravene the Act of Parliament.

That the restriction will be the means of inflicting great hardship upon persons who may wish to transmit the produce of their industry from one part of the country to another, as "goods sent for sale or in execution of an order," and cause annoyance and inconvenience to thousands daily who may wish to transmit trifling articles which are not "*bonâ fide* patterns or samples of merchandise," but may be purchases, gifts, articles required from home, or left behind, &c., &c.

That for these and other reasons, and wholly independent of the bearing which this regulation has, as a retrograde movement, upon the larger question recently brought under your lordship's notice, your memorialists venture earnestly to urge upon your consideration the propriety of cancelling the said restriction, and thus allowing all parcels to pass through the post subject only to the general regulations as to the transmission and postage of such packets.

The remark made in the minute book of the committee, February, 1870, runs: "From what transpired when the deputation waited upon the Postmaster-General, the committee believe that the regulations will be rescinded, and a *bonâ fide* small parcel post substituted for the present restricted pattern post, and that the practice of sending small parcels by what was technically termed 'pattern post' will be officially recognised."

On the 10th May, the following letter was addressed by the committee to a Manchester paper on the subject of the pattern post:—

PATTERN AND SAMPLE POST.
MANCHESTER HOME-TRADE ASSOCIATION.
To the Editor of the "Examiner and Times."

Sir,—It is with some surprise that we notice the letter of the Secretary of the Liverpool Chamber of Commerce to the Postmaster-General, dated the 8th inst., and copied into your paper of this morning. The postal regulations of the 1st October last converted what had previously been practically a parcel post into a mere "sample and pattern post," and in reply to an application to join us in the deputation to urge the postmaster to rescind these regulations, we received the following letter from the secretary of the Liverpool Chamber of Commerce:—

"Chamber of Commerce, Liverpool, 15th February, 1871.

"Dear Sir,—I am directed by the council to inform you that they have had your communication of the 2nd December before them, and to say that they *regret that the facilities hitherto afforded by the pattern post should recently have been restricted to the conveyance of packages of samples and patterns without value,* but consider that the question is one mainly affecting the retail trades of the country.

"I am, dear sir, yours respectfully,
"WILLIAM BLOOD, Secretary.
"The President, Vice-President, and Hon. Secretary of the Manchester Home-Trade Association."

The Liverpool Chamber of Commerce now appears to have reversed its opinion, as the secretary says, in his letter of the 8th inst.: "The Chamber beg also respectfully to point out that the abolition of the sample and pattern post is wholly gratuitous and uncalled for either by public opinion or by fiscal necessity. So far from its abolition being demanded by public opinion, *it is the one department of the post-office which has given the greatest satisfaction to traders;* and while there have been many proposals for its extension, there have been none for its abolition."

And instead of the question being "one mainly affecting the retail trades of the country," and therefore not calling for the special notice of the Liverpool Chamber, it is now asserted "that the sample post has stimulated, and in many cases has called into existence, important departments of commercial activity; and each successive reduction of charge and increase of accommodation has been followed by an immediate expansion of the inland trade of the country."

Now, our opposition to the regulations of the* 1st of October last is based upon the fact that, instead of being an "increase of accommodation," they established a vexatious restriction, which deprived the public of nine-tenths of the value of the pre-existing arrangements; and in this view we were supported by nearly all the Chambers of Commerce in the kingdom.

The object of the bill introduced into Parliament by the Postmaster-General is to change the merely pattern and sample post into a *bonâ fide* parcel post within the limit of twelve ounces, at a scale of charges to be arranged by Treasury order, and, of course, subject to modification from time to time, at the discretion of the Lords of the Treasury.

It is quite true the proposed unit of charge is a penny instead of a halfpenny, as heretofore, but it is equally true that the unit of weight for a penny letter will be raised from half an ounce to one ounce, and we submit that the public, particularly the commercial public, will be largely the gainers by the change,† and the privilege of transmitting all packets "closed" will be highly valued.

---

* Sec. 10, page 12. The postage is now one halfpenny for every weight of two ounces or fraction thereof; but the pattern or sample post is restricted to *bonâ fide* trade patterns or samples of merchandise. Goods sent for sale, or in execution of an order (however small the quantity may be), or any articles sent by one private individual to another, which are not actually patterns or samples, are not admissible.

† The following scale shows the extent of this change:—

Not exceeding

Existing letter rate	½oz.	1oz.	1½	2	2½	3	3½	4	4½	5	5½	6
	1d.	2d.	3d.	4d.	5d.	6d.	7d.	8d.	9d.	10d.	11d.	12d.

Proposed rate 1d.   1½d.   2d.   2½d.

Existing letter rate	6½	7	7½	8	8½	9	9½	10	10½	11	11½	12
	13d.	14d.	15d.	16d.	17d.	18d.	19d.	20d.	21d.	22d.	23d.	24d.

Proposed rate   3d.   3½d.   4d.

Moreover, it is obvious to all who have paid any serious attention to the question that the vexatious distinction between open and closed packets, which was the real difficulty in the way of the recognition of a parcel post, and the ground for the restriction of such post by the regulations of October 1st to *bonâ fide* trade patterns or samples of merchandise not having any saleable value, cannot be abolished without either reducing the unit of the letter rate to a halfpenny, or commencing the parcel scale at a penny. They must be uniform throughout if the penny letter is to be protected.

We are quite willing, when the time arrives for deciding the scale, to join the Liverpool Chamber of Commerce in pressing upon the Postmaster-General the propriety of carrying the penny rate up to two ounces instead of one ounce (which is what we understood he originally intended), but this is a very different question from opposing the attempt which he is now making to amend the law so as to convert a restricted pattern and sample post into a *bonâ fide* and openly recognised parcel post, leaving the scale of charges to be varied from time to time as occasion may require.

Since that date the postal authorities have made most important changes, *e.g.*, in reference to the half-penny cards, the weight allowed in closed envelopes for one penny, the introduction of sixpenny telegrams, and the important and invaluable privilege of parcels post for parcels up to seven pounds weight; the latter a revolution almost as great as that wrought by Rowland Hill, and which, like the penny postage, will go on increasing in usefulness, affording facilities and benefits both in private and commercial life. In the matter of the sixpenny telegrams, a memorial was sent from the association to the Postmaster-General, in view of the uncertainty of the bill becoming law during that session of Parliament, urging the importance of its early passage; and a promise was received, in reply, from Lord John Manners, to give attention to the suggestions accompanying the memorial.

So far back as January, 1880, the subject of greater
facilities for commercial travellers was being agitated
by the association. Each of the railway companies
was approached by letter on the subject; the substance
of which was that the various mercantile firms of
London, Birmingham, and Manchester now required
for their business a much larger number of travellers,
each with a greatly increased variety of patterns, and
the request was made "that in future each commercial
should be allowed to carry patterns and samples as
follows: If travelling first class, four hundredweight;
second class, three hundredweight; third class, two
hundredweight; to be excessed above this limit up to
two hundredweight at the rate of one halfpenny per
mile."*   In the very next month a reply was received
from the superintendent of the London and North-
Western Railway Company announcing important
concessions. Free conveyance was to be allowed to
commercial travellers of double the amount of luggage
allowed to ordinary passengers, according to the class
of carriage in which they travelled; and any weight of
luggage over this amount would be conveyed at one-
half the usual rate, no excess charge being made of
less than one shilling.

Early and resolute action was also taken by the
association when, during the parliamentary session of
1884-5, nine of the principal railway companies introduced bills to the House of Commons for the purpose
of revising and extending their powers in respect of

---

* See address delivered at Crewe, January, 1880, page 166.

charges for the carriage of goods.   In these bills the companies sought the power to "add to the prescribed rates a reasonable sum, (1) in respect of the cost of and expense at terminal stations; and (2) in respect of loading, unloading, providing covers, covering and uncovering, collection and delivery, and any service incidental to the duty or business of a carrier, where any such service is performed by the company."   Each bill contained the definition of the words "terminal station."   "The expression 'terminal station' shall mean and include any station or siding or place at which merchandise traffic is received from or delivered to the consignor or consignee thereof."   It was evident that if these terminal charges were granted it would probably largely increase the total cost of transit.   The railway commissioners had hitherto refused to allow the companies to charge "terminals" in all actions that had been tried before them.   It was, moreover, an obvious objection to the new bills that there would be no settled basis for charges, and that, as a result, private individuals would have to bear the expense of litigation in ascertaining what were "reasonable charges."   It was decided that the committee of the Home-Trade Association should draw up a petition, which should be sent to Mr. Jacob Bright, M.P., for presentation in the House of Commons.   The petition referring to the bills introduced into the House by the railway companies stated :—

That the said bills propose to authorise the said companies to charge undefined sums in addition to the maximum rates for the cost of and expenses incurred at stations, thereby introducing a principle at variance with the uniform practice of Parliament in fixing maximum rates, and imposing upon traders an unjustifiable expense in litigation in order to ascertain the amount legally chargeable for the conveyance of goods and cattle, and practically rendering the maximum rates useless and no longer a protection to the public using the said railways.

That the said bills propose to increase the maximum rates on almost every article specified in the various Acts upon the faith of which the powers granted to the several companies have been bestowed by Parliament and contain numerous provisions of an injurious character.

That the attempts of the said companies so to add to the burdens of agriculture and trade are unwarrantable and a violation of the public faith in the Acts of the several companies, in reliance upon which numerous works have been built and vast expenditure incurred by traders and others, and that, if the said bills pass into law, new burdens will be imposed upon the industry and agriculture of the country with disastrous consequences to the welfare of this country.

Your petitioners, therefore, humbly pray your honourable House that the said bills may not pass into law.

Not only was the prejudicial effect upon nearly all classes of common goods of any increase in charges distinctly realised and stated to Mr. Bright in commending the petition to his support, but also the novel principle that would be introduced into railway legislation if these bills became law, inasmuch as in all previous powers granted to railway companies by the Legislature, all maximum charges were fully and clearly stated. Copies of the petition were sent also to the other borough members, Messrs. Slagg and Houldsworth, asking them to support Mr. Bright.*

---

* One is reminded in this connection of the fight to get the railway people to reduce the insurance on silk, which lasted a considerable time. The Carriers Act passed years before was still in force, under which they are protected against loss on any parcel of silk goods beyond the value

Another of the important questions brought before the Home-Trade Association, and with regard to which active steps have more than once been taken, is that of the Bankruptcy Laws. Mr. Chamberlain's Bankruptcy Bill of 1881 was carefully reviewed by the committee, assisted by their solicitor, Mr. Craven, and a deputation to the Board of Trade, appointed to represent the association. A number of "remarks and suggestions" were printed and circulated by the committee, bearing upon the new bill. The freedom of the creditors, to whom the property of a bankrupt exclusively belongs, was shown to be desirable, in determining alike the mode of administration, and the parties to administer, not precluding, however, the necessity of a certain amount of supervision and control. The need for a provision whereby an adverse

---

of £10; merchants were put to great straits sometimes to know what to do; the insurance and carriage rate were oppressive.

In order to bring the absurdity of the charge home to the railway authorities, an opportunity was watched for, when there should be a fair sized parcel, the value of which was sufficient to warrant an experiment.

Very soon a customer came in from a large town and bought about £200 of silks. And instead of sending the goods in the usual course, and paying the high class rate for carriage together with the insurance charge, it was decided to send two men with the goods, and it was found, after paying all expenses for refreshments, wages, and fares, there was a considerable saving effected—the company having carried two men in addition to the parcels.

This circumstance, coupled with the representations made by different houses, had much to do with getting the insurance rate reduced, first to 10s., then to 5s., and now, for some time passed, the rate has been 1s. per cent; and if I am correctly informed, the railway companies receive more money at that rate than under any previous charge.

Act of Bankruptcy might be more speedily obtained, as under the proposed bill, there would be a delay of twenty-six or twenty-seven days was suggested; the opinion was strongly expressed that when the petition is presented by the debtor, it should be presented in the district where the largest amount of the trade creditors carry on business, and, if presented by a creditor, he should be at liberty to present it in the district where the creditor carries on business; that, in any case immediately on the list of creditors being filed, and it being ascertained where the largest amount of trade debts is owing, the meeting should be called for and held in that town, and the proceedings transferred to the court of that district, but the creditors shall have power to transfer, by resolution, the proceedings to any district they might elect. The committee of the association expressed themselves of opinion that the working of late acts had tended to the prejudice of creditors, whereas it ought always to be borne in mind that they are the sufferers and the parties aggrieved; and suggested that provisions should be introduced into the bill by which the creditors should have greater facilities of seeking the assistance and advice of the court, and of bringing their special grievances and complaints before it without incurring the risk of having to pay costs, with some special exceptions.

Whilst the Bankruptcy Act of 1883 was under discussion, three memorials were addressed to the Right Honourable Joseph Chamberlain, as President of the Board of Trade, the first referring to the bill in its more general aspects, the second to the clauses relating to Ireland, and the third to clause 122. As they furnish good examples of the steps the association has taken with respect to measures of great importance to traders, copies of these memorials, together with copy of a memorial sent in 1884, suggesting amendments to the said Act of 1883, are here given:—

To the Right Honourable Joseph Chamberlain, M.P., President of the Board of Trade.

We, the undersigned, being the committee of the Home-Trade Association of the city of Manchester, desire respectfully to draw your attention to the following suggestions in relation to the Bankruptcy Act of 1883. We venture to hope that they may be taken into your consideration with a view to the introduction into any bill to amend the said Act of such clauses as will effect the changes herein proposed as necessary to the satisfactory working of the new procedure:—

1. Prior to the first of January, one thousand eight hundred and eighty-four, it has been the practice in the home trade of Manchester to have proofs of debt sworn before a justice of the peace, who has attended at the office of this association on one day in each week for that purpose. In consequence of the operation of section 135 of the new Act, a justice of the peace in England is disqualified from having such proofs sworn before him. Inconvenience and expense are thus caused to creditors without any corresponding advantage to the community. We submit that the office of a justice of the peace is in itself a sufficient guarantee of the fitness of the holder thereof to administer oaths for the above purpose.

2. Great inconvenience is caused by reason of the provision in the new Act that every insertion in a proxy shall be in the handwriting of the person giving the same. We submit that it should be competent for a creditor to sign a proxy which has been previously completed by a person in his regular employ.

3. It is often impossible to ascertain prior to a meeting of creditors the nature of the specific resolutions which will be considered, and on that ground we suggest that a special proxy should entitle the person holding the same to vote generally upon any resolution which may be

submitted to such meeting, limiting it only to the particular meeting in respect of which it is given or any adjournment thereof.

4. In many cases, either for the purpose of carrying on the debtor's business, or of obtaining advances, or because of the amount of the cash balances, it is desirable that the trustee should have an account with a local bank, and we submit that the fee of three pounds for and incidental to the order of the Board of Trade for that purpose should be reduced to one pound one shilling.

5. The charge of six pounds per cent on the net assets realised by the official receiver is excessive in cases where such assets exceed one thousand pounds. It appears to us that a graduated scale should be adopted for his remuneration, with a rate of percentage diminishing with every five thousand pounds up to eleven thousand pounds, but being in no case less than two pounds per cent.

For example : Assets up to one thousand pounds—six pounds per cent.

Assets from one thousand pounds up to six thousand pounds: Six pounds per cent on the first one thousand pounds and four pounds per cent on the surplus.

Assets from six thousand pounds to eleven thousand pounds: Six pounds per cent on the first one thousand; four pounds per cent from one thousand pounds up to six thousand pounds, and three pounds per cent on the surplus.

Assets exceeding eleven thousand pounds : Six pounds per cent on the first one thousand pounds ; four pounds per cent from one thousand pounds up to six thousand pounds; three pounds per cent from six thousand pounds up to eleven thousand pounds, and two pounds per cent on the surplus.

6. We submit that the majority of the creditors in any bankruptcy should have the right of selecting the court in which the bankruptcy proceedings shall be conducted without the necessity of previously obtaining the certificate of a judge or registrar.

THE MEMORIAL OF THE HOME-TRADE ASSOCIATION, MANCHESTER.

To the Right Honourable Joseph Chamberlain.

Your memorialists are largely engaged in trade with Ireland, and deeply interested in the bankruptcy system of that country.

Having regard to the different circumstances affecting trade as between Ireland and England, and to the different system of Bankruptcy Law prevailing in Ireland from that proposed to be remedied in England, and also to the fact that your memorialists, who will be vitally affected by any alteration in the Irish bankruptcy system, have not had any opportunity of considering the clauses relating to Ireland proposed to be added to the Bankruptcy Bill, your memorialists are strongly of opinion that it is most undesirable that the clauses relating to Ireland should (at least for the present) be passed into law.

Your memorialists have no doubt that if opportunity were afforded the opinion of your memorialists would be shared by other centres interested in trade in Ireland.

Your memorialists therefore pray that the view of your memorialists may be taken into consideration, and that the proposed clauses relating to Ireland may not be proceeded with.

To the Right Honourable Joseph Chamberlain.

Your memorialists humbly desire to bring before your notice the effects of clause 122, subsection 4, of the proposed Bankruptcy Bill now before Parliament, and to express their opinion that the amount of £20 named in such clause as the extent to which goods shall be protected from seizure should be reduced to £10; but, fearing that such amount of £20 will be still retained, they beg strongly to urge that provision shall be added to such clause, deferring its operation until a period of twelve months shall have expired after the Act comes into operation, to afford creditors of small debtors the opportunity of obtaining payment of debts incurred before the Act comes into operation, as otherwise the results of this clause may be most disastrous to existing creditors, whose interests as such is represented at £200,000,000 sterling.

No labour has been spared to render the association an efficient factor in the handling of questions affecting trade. The County Court Bills and Bills of Sale Act have been the subjects of discussion and of deputations to Government officials. The writer has no hesitation in expressing his belief that much has been done in the interests of the trading community at large, and of the home trade in particular, and that it is owing to the assiduous and continuous attention of this association, which represents the home-trade houses of Manchester, that they have been free from the disgraceful and disreputable results of winding up estates which have occurred in other branches of trade.   If all the various sections of traders would pay as much personal attention to these matters as is paid by the home-trade houses, neither Judge Jordan nor any other judge would be able to say that "if the creditors knew what was done under assignments, there would be no more assignments made."   At any rate, the opinion of the before-named gentleman is altogether at variance with the experience of the writer, who holds to the opinion of Lord Hatherley, which he expressed to a deputation from the Manchester Home-Trade Association, at which the writer was present, in reference to a bill he was bringing into the House of Lords: "There can be no doubt that where the creditors will take pains to look after estates and those who administer them, they ought to know what is best to be done, and matters should be left in their hands."

A few years ago, we had several cases of fraud in connection with the home trade.   Two or three fraudulent debtors had been prosecuted.   Good as this was felt to be for the trade, it was a very expensive process for the individual houses, and, after due consideration, it was resolved by the association that a fund should be established, out of which the expense of a prosecution (when that action was approved by the committee) should be paid.   Application was made to the different houses, and in a very few days guarantees were given to the extent of £10,000.

The fact was made known pretty widely that, in any well-authenticated case of fraud by a draper, the association would prosecute, and there is reason to believe it had a considerable influence for good, though it is just to add that this branch of the country's trade will bear comparison with any other class of traders in this respect.

When, however, cases of insolvency are brought before the Home-Trade Association, it is often curious to watch the men and listen to their excuses. One has had a bad wife or bad children, another has been robbed by servants, a third has made some error in judgment; but when it comes to the test of figures, disaster is very often to be traced to the fact of the trader's incapacity or neglect, and his statements as to profits and expenses are utterly at variance with all intelligent experience; and the only proper thing to do is to take the estate out of his hands and wind it up.

The debtor sometimes comes forward asserting that he has done his best, and is greatly distressed at the state of his affairs; the estate is there, however, and if the creditors do not like to accept seven shillings and sixpence in the pound, of course they must wind up; he can do no more. His solicitor is present to vouch for the accuracy of all his statements. When the debtor is asked for a copy of his last stock-taking sheets, he cannot produce one; but one of the creditors has a copy which the debtor had given him six months previously, and it is read.

"Yes," he says, "that is something like it, but trade

has been indifferent since then, and I must have taken a rosy view of things; some of the book debts have turned out bad."

"But, allowing for all this, there is still a deficiency of £700 to be accounted for."

"Well, I can't help it," he rejoins. When he is asked if he will make an assignment, his solicitor at once says "No." "Will the debtor allow an accountant to go and examine the stock and books, and report to a further meeting?" is then asked. After some hesitation, this is agreed to. The accountant goes to the debtor's place of business, checks the stock and debts, ascertains the liabilities, finds out from his books that he has bought so much during the past six months, adds this to the stock, then finds out, as nearly as he can, the receipts during the same period, with the result that a large deficiency is shown, which cannot be accounted for.

Being an experienced man, and knowing something of human frailties, the accountant takes a walk round the sitting-room and bedrooms. He finds in the bedroom that one part has been somewhat recently whitewashed, and in the sitting-room he finds no cupboard in the corner as there usually is, and there is no opening under the stairs. By tapping the wall of the sitting-room, he finds some boarding in it; he has it uncovered, and there discovers a large cupboard full of good linens, silks, &c. He next gets under the stairs, and finds more stock there. He then has the ceiling broken upstairs, and a still further quantity of goods is brought to light. The result is that the deficiency is turned into a surplus; the creditors are paid in full, and the man is put in prison.

Another case turns up, where the losses of the debtor can be fairly traced. Had it not been for sickness and trouble, which the man had no power to avert, he would not have been in his sad position.

In such cases the writer has occasionally seen the creditors torture the man with hard words, and try to wring the last shilling out of him, but as a rule the honest and good man is leniently dealt with, and the adjudication is fairly made upon the merits of the case.

The committee of the Home-Trade Association has always numbered amongst its members some of the most representative men in the trade. It has had a series of presidents, only two of whom survive, Mr. Philip Gillibrand and Mr. Reuben Spencer; and we cannot allow the opportunity to pass without making reference to Mr. Gillibrand, who rendered very important and valuable service to the trading interests of this city during the period of his membership, and especially when he occupied the chair. He had large experience and capacity combined with urbanity of nature and great courtesy, which made him respected and esteemed by all, and we earnestly and sincerely hope he may long be spared to enjoy his well-earned rest.

THE COMMERCIAL TRAVELLERS' ASSOCIATION.

The experience of the writer in connection with the latter has served to heighten his appreciation of the ability and foresight of the members, who have been

H

justly termed " the ambassadors of commerce." Not only are the duties they discharge as representatives of their respective firms responsible and onerous, but they wield a considerable influence as the trusted counsellors of the tradesmen they visit. Over and above their business routine of exhibiting patterns and booking orders, the most delicate and important matters are often referred to them for advice, such as the commercial interests of the tradesman, *e.g.*, the special departments of his business he should cultivate or discontinue, the placing a son or a daughter in a school or a situation, the transfer of young men to other situations, sometimes even the removal of a business to another part of the same town or to a different town altogether. There are few positions in which a capable and judicious man can be of more practical service to his fellow traders; many drapers of good standing would at once admit that they owe their position almost entirely to the assistance and guidance of some commercial traveller.

The association which these gentlemen have established for united action in matters affecting trade, and particularly affecting themselves as a body, has been of considerable service in securing advantages to the members and to commercial men as a whole. Much attention is given to the discussion and presentation of such just and reasonable claims as the issue by the various railway companies of cheap week-end tickets to *bonâ fide* travellers, available for the whole year, so that every commercial traveller, if he so desires, shall be able to visit his home at least once a week at a

moderate cost. This end would be already gained in
the case of those whose daily duties are within comparatively short distance of the trading centre if
the railway companies would issue, as has been
suggested by the Commercial Travellers' Association,
circular season tickets, *i.e.,* tickets available for the
whole year upon any line and to any place within
such mileage as shall be stated on the ticket from
the centre at which they are issued. The proposal
is very clearly stated in *The Mail Train* for January
21st, 1885: "Thus, for instance, if we take Manchester as an example, the Lancashire and Yorkshire,
London and North-Western, Manchester, Sheffield
and Lincolnshire, and Midland would, we presume, be
the contracting companies. Therefore, what a commercial man would have to do would be to look what
was the extreme distance of his journey in either
direction, and then ascertain the mileage, and at the
rate of twenty shillings per mile per annum first-class,
we suggest he should be entitled to have such a ticket
covering any number of miles in any direction round
Manchester. The ticket would simply require to have
marked on it the name of the maximum distance
station on each of the lines of rails which run out from
Manchester, and all places within that would be available to the ticket, the companies dividing the amount
received for the ticket in exact proportion to the
aggregate mileage covered by their trains in a straight
direction from the central point. This would be an
extremely simple arrangement, and one that would
work most advantageously for the holder, as in taking

the ticket out he would see what distance would meet his wants best, and include the largest amount of working ground; then, if in one direction his towns were more sparse and scattered, he would simply pay the excess fare between the station his ticket was available and the extreme point for, and the extra distance he may desire to go to. And there could not be the slightest trouble about such an arrangement, as each ticket would clearly indicate the maximum-distance station in every direction, and anything beyond would simply require to be paid for as used, the annual ticket being the guarantee for the man up to a certain point. Then these tickets should only be issued first-class, and thus materially relieve the pressure on the third-class space, and the commercial would have all the additional comfort for what he is at present paying for third-class accommodation. The result to the railway companies would be a positive utilisation of the large number of first-class carriages they run out from large centres at present almost empty in the mornings, and back at night in a similar state, the commercial men filling them up on the return journeys when the ordinary suburban traffic does not require them. This would more equally distribute their passengers, and, again, what is of vast importance, place at once in their hands an enormous sum of money down for such tickets, these being paid for in advance, and the interest alone on the money would be no trifle.

If this were arranged as a means of providing with greater facilities for enjoying home life those who travel within comparatively limited areas, it would be but one step to the granting of a further concession for the sake of those who travel to greater distances, and at present find the cost of returning home for the week end burdensome.

Another desideratum is a reduction in the charge for parcels left in the cloak rooms of the railway stations, for a day or part of a day, from twopence to a penny per parcel. In the matter of extending the amount of luggage allowed to each traveller, too, the railway authorities have been memorialised by the Travellers' Association, both in conjunction with other associations and independently of them. As an example, portions of a memorial sent to the United Meeting of Representatives of English Railway Companies, held November 11th, 1880, may be quoted. With a view to showing that the previous concessions, already referred to in this chapter, arising from the joint action of the Manchester Home-Trade Association, the Commercial Travellers' Association, and the Wholesale Drapery and Textile Trades of the City of London, had been beneficial to the railway companies as well as to travellers, the facts were stated:—

"1. The additional facilities for carrying heavy weights of samples have caused an increase in the number of persons travelling with samples; many of the large houses sending out special travellers from the different departments more frequently than formerly.

"2. Many commercial travellers, in order to avoid paying the excess charge for their luggage, now travel in a higher class than that formerly used.

"3. That the heavy restrictions previously imposed

with respect to the carrying of samples caused many travellers to discontinue the use of the railways, and to drive over their districts. The concessions given by the railway companies have induced many of these travellers to return again to the railway."

The memorial goes on to say that had the concession asked for been granted (viz., 4 cwt. first class, 3 cwt. second class, 2 cwt. third class), "the pecuniary benefit to the different companies would have been greater than it has been."

The attention of the Board is called to the granting of other important facilities detailed in the memorial: (*a*) The adoption of a cheque system, such as that found to work so well in America, as insuring the greatest safety to the travellers in respect of loss of luggage and delay in obtaining the same, at a very small inconvenience and cost to the companies. (*b*) The desirability of establishing a separate luggage compartment for commercial travellers' sample cases, as considerable damage sometimes results to the cases from the miscellaneous nature of the contents of the luggage van, especially during the tourist seasons, as well as delay and inconvenience to the traffic. (*c*) The matter already referred to is petitioned for, viz., the issue of return tickets to commercial travellers, to extend from the Friday to the Monday at a single fare; the guarantee of good faith to be the possession of a certificate of membership of the Commercial Travellers' Association.

Enough has been quoted to show the kind of action taken by the association and the importance of its deliberations. The reasonableness of the concessions demanded is manifest. The travellers are the very backbone of the railway traffic, and since their labours are beneficial both to railway companies and the merchants they represent, the cost should be more evenly divided, the companies sharing or at least lightening the expenses of travel. With regard to luggage, clearly no commercial will for his own pleasure increase its amount; his first and foremost thought is to reduce it so far as he can consistently with his business requirements. The only possible temptation he can have is that of adding new patterns to his samples, by which he hopes to secure larger and more numerous orders, and then if he accomplishes his purpose the railway company is sure to profit by it.

CHAPTER V.

PROVIDENT AND BENEVOLENT
SOCIETIES.

FEW objects are more desirable and more worthy of hearty encouragement and support than the provident and benevolent associations of the various classes of workers. The Warehousemen and Clerks' Provident Association, the Commercial Travellers' Benevolent Association, the Warehousemen and Clerks' Schools, Porters' and Packers' Benevolent Societies, are institutions so important and valuable, both to the members themselves and to the trades in which they are engaged, as to merit the careful attention and active co-operation of commercial houses and of all interested in the welfare of the workers.

The Commercial Travellers' Benevolent Association, for instance, is an institution originated by the wisdom and foresight of the gentlemen travelling for our firms. Their duties, alike onerous and honourable, are efficiently discharged, and the value to the trade of the country of the services of this body of 40,000 men can scarcely be estimated. The great majority of them believe in and act up to the principle laid down by one of our leaders—"I hate to see anything done by halves; if it be right, do it boldly and well." They know, and act as knowing, that there is no substitute for thorough-going earnestness and ardour, and many succeed, as they desire, in making provision for old age, believing it their duty, as one of our writers says, to "get out of the scrape of being alive and *poor*." But there are in all large communities men who cannot successfully compete with others in the same field, and who fail to realise in their business or occupation the results which their industry and integrity of purpose have merited. There is always a certain section of society, and of every class of society, who, from misfortune, ill-health, or other adverse circumstances, become incapable of continuing their services ; it is therefore incumbent upon them to try by combination to prepare for adverse times. What man knows whether a sad fatality may overtake him, brought about by no fault of his own ? It should be regarded by every traveller as a duty and a privilege to join the association for mutual help; and all merchants should be glad to assist them in this grand project of combination for the good of those that may be unfortunate.

There are three duties which are paramount, in the writer's opinion : every traveller ought to insure his life, to subscribe to the schools, and to be a member of the benevolent association. One should feel that by saying " I shall look after myself, and leave the others to do the same," he is depriving himself of a high privilege and forfeiting the real enjoyment which comes from helping those who are less fortunate than himself, not to say that, if he is a married man, he is neglecting one of the most sacred obligations of life resting upon him—namely, of protecting from poverty and suffering and possible degradation those that are the nearest to him in claim, dependence, and affection.

To fail in this duty is to fail to retain the full power
and honour of manhood.

· The next and one of first importance is the Manchester Warehousemen and Clerks' Provident Association.
It was established for the purpose of assisting warehouse men and clerks in time of sickness and distress,
and also to provide means of sustenance for those who
might become incapacitated for business by accident,
or by physical or mental disease; to provide a certain
amount of money payable at the death of a member,
and for the funeral expenses of members' wives. The
association has rooms admirably adapted for club life,
containing a library, and affording opportunities for
reading the newspapers and periodicals, and for inter-
· course with fellow-workers. Institutions of this kind
are helpful in many ways. They encourage and
cultivate habits of thrift, economy, and thoughtfulness,
and bring about friendships and associations of a
higher class and better character than those formed in
many other places, over and above the help they
render in case of sickness and depression of trade.
The broad and safe basis, on which the association
is established, is attested by the fact that it has now
existed for more than thirty years, and has made continuous progress; it has won the sympathy and secured
the administrative ability of some of the best known
business men of the city and district. An important
sphere of the society's usefulness is the assistance it
gives to young men seeking new fields of labour; and
the steady increase in the ordinary subscriptions from
members shows that young men are alive to the

advantages the society offers. The helpfulness of the association is scarcely to be computed by the amount of actual disbursement; it is rather to be found in the experience and feelings of the recipients of the help afforded at times when it is most needed. Occasionally there may be an undeserving case upon the books, but this is altogether outweighed by the thousand good and true men, whose lives have been made more tolerable by the assistance received from the association. An intelligent and manly interest is taken by the members in the proceedings of the association, proving the confidence of the associates in the organisation. A fuller account of the institution and its work is given in the following address, delivered by the writer at the thirty-second annual meeting of the association, held in the Lecture Hall of the Manchester Athenæum, February 22nd, 1888:—

I have always looked forward to these annual gatherings with pleasure, because I have the opportunity of meeting with, and saying a few words to, many of my fellow-workers who are engaged in the great duty of providing and distributing the materials which contribute so much to the comfort of mankind in every country; and, speaking particularly of the textile branch of business in which many of us are employed, we all know it assists largely in cultivating public taste, in stimulating the genius of the mechanic, and in developing various branches of manufacture. It seeks to adorn that finest and grandest of all structures, the human frame. In far-off lands, where civilisation has not reached, you read of men and women living and moving about in an almost nude state, but when once the British trader visits them and shows his productions, desire for our fabrics is very soon kindled, and the output of our looms and spindles is sought after. The taste once created grows rapidly, and the refining influence of appropriate dress is seen and felt throughout the whole population of the countries into which it is introduced. I must not, however, dwell further upon this at present.

Turning to the report which your worthy secretary has read, we are told that the prosperity of your society has been more marked in the year 1887 than in any year since its establishment. You have three branches in this great association, viz., the general fund, the benevolent or annuity fund, the burial fund, and in each you have a large surplus of profit; and, what is perhaps more pleasing to know, your ratio of expense has fallen so as to show a margin of nearly £300 within the prescribed limits. The great difficulty with traders at the present time, especially merchants and manufacturers, is to keep expenses down—the tendency everywhere is to increase. You may maintain or even increase the volume of trade, but the profits are smaller, whilst the expenses are larger. I must now ask you to allow me the opportunity of making a few observations, not only upon the present condition of your society, but as to the rate of progress which has been made since 1880. I have had the assistance of your secretary in taking out the following figures:—

Subscriptions in 1880 amounted to	...	...	...	£1,752
,,	1881	,,	... ...	1,764
,,	1882	,,	... ...	1,868
,,	1883	,,	... ...	2,000
,,	1884	,,	... ...	2,343
,,	1885	,,	... ...	2,772
,,	1886	,,	... ...	3,058
,,	1887	,,	... ...	3,251

Showing an increase of £4,040 in subscriptions in the last four years over the preceding four years.

The number of subscribing members in 1883 was one thousand five hundred and fifty, in 1887 two thousand five hundred and sixty-five, an increase of one thousand and fifteen.

The total profit your society made during the four years ending December 31st last was £3,807, and of this no less than £1,230 was the profit for 1887.

Out of the numerous situations offered to your members during the last four years three hundred and thirty-seven were accepted, and only twenty-six members were out of work a month ago. This, I think, is one of the most cheering statements which appears in your report.

The total assets of your association have risen from £13,938 in 1883 to £17,878 at the date of your last balance sheet. These assets may appear large to some, and the question may be asked " Why build up this reserve?" Gentlemen, there is a very sufficient answer to that enquiry. Your membership has greatly increased of late years, I might say it has gone up by leaps and bounds, and I believe the time is not very distant when your constituency will be five thousand instead of two thousand five hundred and sixty-five, and then will come your testing time, when the old members, so largely increased in number and age, will be entitled to the extended benefits. That is to say, any member who has been on the books for ten years, and has not been a claimant, will, under the amended rules, be entitled to two extra weeks' allowance at £1 per week, and after fifteen years' membership, four extra weeks at £1 per week. After twenty years an extra six weeks at the same rate; and after twenty-five years, eight weeks' additional grant. One more item and I have done with figures. Your books show disbursements to members since 1855 amounting to £26,700, and for medical fees £10,000, or a grand total of £36,800. About the receipts: I can quite conceive it may have been very difficult for some of you, in special times of pressure, and under trying circumstances, arising from various causes, to continue to pay up your subscriptions promptly; but, on the other side, I cannot command language which can satisfactorily express my own feelings, or which can convey to this audience an adequate idea of the great relief and joy which the distribution of such a large amount of money has afforded to the various members and families to whom it has been sent. Your board now propose to make a further departure from the old lines, and from this date to give the members the advantage of the professional services of a chiropodist at half his usual fees. You have now only to become subscribers to our dental hospital of such an amount as shall enable the members to take advantage of the services which can be rendered to them by that important institution, which has upon its staff some of the first dentists of this county, I might almost say of this country, and this being done, your roll will be complete, provision being made to meet nearly all the wants which poor human nature is heir to. You have a library and reading-room, and facilities for cultivating social life under the most favourable circumstances. You provide your members with monetary help in case of distress; you meet their requirements in times of sickness and pain, by affording them the best medical advice; you come to their rescue when old age and incapacity for continued labour overtakes them; you discharge the last obligations under which they can place the association by finding the necessary means for an interment suitable to their station.

I think you will agree with me that your present position warrants me in saying that if at any time during the past few years you have had reason to rejoice because of the new departure you made in the year 1883, it is now.   The wisdom of taking offices in a prominent position and appointing a secretary, whose whole time should be devoted to your service, has been demonstrated beyond all question.   You must allow me to say that the board deserves the warmest approval of every member for their action in the two matters named.   The society has passed through all the trials and small indispositions or afflictions which attend infancy and youth; it has now arrived at manhood and is strong, and capable of bearing great burdens.   Your funds are well and safely invested.   I sincerely trust that the just reward of your steady perseverance, the fidelity of your officers, and of your members may extend your powers for good work in every department, and that from solicitors, bankers, accountants, merchants, and manufacturers, the enquiries for young men to fill vacancies may continually increase, and so find employment for all your members.

Now let me say a few words through the press, which, as you know, is the most powerful medium at our command for reaching and touching the public mind upon any subject, and also let me speak through you who are present this evening, to the young men of this city and district, and especially those recently married, who as yet have not enrolled themselves as members of this useful society.   They know from observation how many are the troubles and anxieties through which employers as well as employed have to pass, how many masters fail to succeed through want of administrative capacity or through want of capital, or in consequence of changes in their business, or it may be the removal from the district of the particular kind of manufacture in which they have been engaged as makers or distributors.   On the other hand, amongst the employés the causes of non-success are as varied; their failure is not unfrequently, in consequence of the total unfitness of the person for warehouse or office life.   Again and again I have seen honest, industrious young men, who, as plumbers, painters, joiners, or mechanics, would have made progress and a satisfactory position, who as clerks or salesmen are totally out of place, and never can succeed in keeping a situation worthy of themselves.

There is a feeling amongst some men (and I make these remarks in all kindness) that there is no necessity for making provision against a bad time or adverse conditions of life. A young man wins the affections of a girl who has been brought up with favourable surroundings, and has known nothing of want or hard labour; by consent of the parents, he marries her and takes her to his own home. For a time matters run smoothly, one or more children are born, and all their income is spent, probably not wisely or necessarily. Through unforeseen and unexpected events, the husband loses his situation and remains unemployed for a time—he is not a member of this or any kindred association. What is the condition of that family? Friends have to be hunted up, humiliation takes the place of manly independence, then comes suffering of mind and body, for which they are all unprepared, least of all the wife and children. Or perhaps the young man dies and the widow has neither the benefit which this association affords to the survivor nor of a life assurance policy, and she and her little ones have to turn out into a hard world to find a living as best they can. Young friends, let me ask you to ponder over this matter, and, remembering the obligations you are under, act like prudent and generous men—play the man.

On all sides, from the Board of Trade reports, from statesmen of the highest rank, from manufacturers and merchants in various districts, we hear the glad news that there is a revival of trade. Some think we have come to the period when we have a right to expect it, because we have passed over more than the usual time of depression. This I will not stop to discuss.

But I sincerely trust that this society may share in the coming prosperity, and be still further enlarged in its membership, and in its funds, and that its beneficent work may be thereby so far increased that the report which we have had read to-night may be but as the twilight and morning warmth preceding the great and fuller light and heat of the mid-day sun. You have the foundations laid of a great organisation capable of doing a noble work; it is for you to see to it that you keep the right men on the board of management, who will wisely administer your funds, and faithfully and energetically carry out the great purposes for which the society was established.

Closely associated in name and object, though an entirely distinct institution, are the Warehousemen and Clerks' Schools. In a large city like Manchester the field of observation before us is large, and one cannot move amongst its population without often being pained to witness the troubles of families from which the head has been taken.   Children are left without home and shelter save where kind hands and hearts set to work to relieve them, and many more would be so but for the invaluable assistance offered by orphanages and schools.   The principles of humanity and brotherhood, of duty, and of Christian love, commend such institutions to the sympathy and support of merchants and business men; and there is surely no more urgent claim upon the members of the class whose children the schools are specially intended to benefit.   The schools are in a high state of efficiency in every department; the health and happiness of the children are cared for; they are brought into frequent contact with members of the committee and other friends who visit the institution, and thus, by wholesome intercourse and broadening influences, the effects of isolation are not felt.   Many are taken to the schools at a very tender age, and one has but to visit the schools to see evidence of the culture and kindness in the midst of which the children are being brought up.   The educational results are likewise of a most encouraging kind.   In many instances boys and girls from these schools will rise to high and useful positions, influencing society for good.   Amongst the girls there may be a Hannah More or a George Eliot; amongst the boys a Martin Luther, a Longfellow, a Bishop Wilberforce, or a Buxton; and all who help on the schools by their subscriptions and active sympathy will be important factors in the results of training given to so many orphan children.

One other benevolent society only shall be mentioned, the Porters' and Packers' Benevolent Society. Association amongst the porters and packers of any large firm is comparatively easy, and gives a membership large enough to be of practical utility. Since 1864 there has been a society of this kind in connection with one large firm; in six years the membership rose from forty-five to two hundred; the present membership is over two hundred. The object of the association is to afford relief in case of distress, sickness, or death amongst its members. The subscription is one penny per week. All benefit or interest in the society ceases in the event of a member leaving the firm from any cause whatever. In case of death, either of a member, his wife, or child, an allowance is made according to the rules. Should the funds accumulate beyond a fixed reserve and the amount required to discharge the claims just referred to, the surplus is equitably divided amongst the members at Christmas. In years when there are a very few or no losses by death, the funds enable the members to provide a good distribution to cheer their families, as well as to enable them to meet other claims which arise at that season of the year. Worthy of very special attention is the investment branch of the association, affording a means whereby members can lay by such a sum as will shortly enable them to secure what is very desirable, a life policy in some insurance society. The expenses of the society, including printing and stationery, are defrayed by the firm, increasing, of course, the dividends paid to the members.

I

CHAPTER VI.

THE LIFE AND DUTIES OF BUSINESS MEN.

IT is a remark one frequently hears in certain society, and often made by professional men, that the life of a business man is a "hum-drum sort of existence," that little or no purpose is served by it other than that of making money. Now, this is altogether at variance with facts. There is a very wide field for thought, energy, and skill in the commercial calling, and associated with it. Trade in its manifold aspects itself affords scope for the highest capacities. It is anything but hum-drum to the intelligent man; ever fresh problems arise which must be solved, contingencies must be provided for, enterprises well directed, and losses made good. Banking, insurance, buying at value, and selling at a profit are practical matters demanding very thoughtful and skilful handling. Then the business man has his duties with respect to trade provident societies to help the unfortunate; there is ever present with him the moral duties of his situation, his word and example affect not only his own honour, but the lives and characters of all around him; the younger employés and apprentices have to be taught the technical niceties and mercantile principles pertaining to the soundest industrial operations; the providing of technical and general schools for the children likely to occupy spheres in the business

world of the next generation is but an extension of the
same duty; besides that the consideration of all public
matters affecting trade directly or indirectly, such as
parliamentary measures, municipal restrictions or development, are well within the sphere of the attention
and in large measure of the control of business men.

Take the manufacturer as an example of these facts.
A manufacturer needs to be a man of mental capacity
and ingenuity; he must buy or construct machinery
suitable for a certain class of work, and must maintain
the same in efficient condition, but to do this requires
a mind of no mean order. He must have skill and
taste in devising new makes of cloth; goods must be
made in new designs, which shall not only meet the
taste of society, but which shall positively create taste.

The goods once made, he must find or make a
market for them. Then arises the necessity for the
proper man to sell the production of his looms and
spindles, and immediately the way is opened up to
that wide field of commercial relation which includes
within its area the traders in the shires of his own
country and the people of distant nations. Then steps
in the question of insurance by land and sea, fire and
marine insurance, and banking arrangements, to facilitate the operation of buying raw products of foreign
lands, and the re-shipping of the manufactured goods.
These operations of buying and selling involve the
employment of capable and industrious men, both at
home and abroad, of clerks and assistants who have to
be familiar with the rates of exchange, as they affect
his foreign trade, and with the rates for discounting in

their own country.   So far, we view the manufacturer in a purely commercial aspect.

But his life and life-influence cover much broader ground.   He is in a position in which many depend upon him for employment, and he is familiar with the fluctuations of trade and the vicissitudes arising from times of dulness and depression in the lives of the workers; as a wise and humane leader of the people's industry, he cannot but see the need of their being helped to provide for adverse times; the various benevolent and provident societies claim his interest and support; so that in questions of maintenance, providence, and social and domestic well-being, he, in some measure almost of necessity, co-operates with those who, in his industrial operations, co-operate with him.   It was entirely without affectation that such large employers of labour as Sir Titus Salt and the late Mr. John Rylands said that they felt upon their shoulders the responsibility of the lives and comforts of the thousands they employed.

True of all men, it is specially true of the business man who comes into close and hourly contact with so many, that " no man liveth unto himself."   Every man is influenced by the stronger mind as unfailingly as the needle by the magnet ; the presence of the weakest has its weight.   On all sides we are touching our fellow-beings, and they are affected for good or evil by what we are, by what we say and do, even by what we think and feel.   Some are built up and strengthened by the unconscious force and influence of others, others are wrenched out of their places and thrown down.

Only by strictest integrity, by habits of personal industry and punctuality, can an influence for good be assured. The order and regularity of the work in a large factory or warehouse, the quiet intelligence with which the whole is conducted, reflect the character of the head of the whole and of the several departments. If a man takes care of his character, his personal influence will take care of itself.

Were business men not predisposed to take in hand the question of general and technical education, the force of circumstances would make it imperative. The competition of the manufacturers of foreign countries, combined with the rapidly developing tastes and corresponding demands of the people, alike force on us the consideration how the capacity for doing good and better work can be developed and increased. The workers must be trained ; and this is a necessity which grows upon us perceptibly with every decade. The broad question of general education, which of course has it due and direct relation to technical education, and to the efficiency of the worker, is happily taken up by the nation and made compulsory. We have abundant evidence of the value and importance of this in the fact that as education extends juvenile crime decreases, and with it the expenses of the police court ; and what is still more cheering the homes of our poorer class of working people are by the direct influence of the children becoming more and more cheerful.

The other sphere of activity, in which the welfare of all business men is brought forward in discussion, and where necessary action taken, has been referred to in the chapter on the home-trade and kindred associations. Whether, therefore, the business man's life and action be considered from the commercial, the philanthropic, the moral, the educational, the industrial, or the social side, it is, if rightly regarded, a noble life, and in it may be developed the highest forces and capacities of a great mind. This may be said, of course, without depreciating in the slightest possible degree the grand callings of ministers of state and of professional men of every grade, and least of all of those who devote their best energy and powers of thought to studying and trying to fathom in some measure the great depths of that wonderful book, the inspiration of which is divine, and fresh from the study of which, their minds aglow with heavenly fire, they go forth to preach and to teach and to uplift man in his aspirations toward a life infinitely transcending in glory and beauty anything attainable on this earth.

Many of the most capable men of business do yet another kind of service in undertaking the duties and responsibilities of municipal life, serving their fellow-citizens in the management of the affairs of the corporation. The importance of such services, gratuitously and often lavishly rendered, it would not be easy to over estimate, the health and very much of the well-being of all the inhabitants of the town or city which they serve being the object of their labours. It is, perhaps, the culminating honour in the life of business men that their conduct, liberality, and intelligence should have so won the respect and confidence of a constituency as that they should be asked to be their representative in the national council at Westminster. But to him who has the fitness for the work and the time at his command it is only second to the parliamentary seat to have a place in the local parliament or council chamber. The duties of a town councillor are of such a character as to benefit the whole of the population within the range of the council's authority. To provide lighting, water, good and well-kept streets, a good sewage system, baths, public parks, and whatever else may minister to the health and happiness of the people, represents a large amount of labour and wise counsel. The first and important duty of the council is not, as some thoughtless people say, to levy rates and taxes; it is far higher, being no less than the devotion of the fruits of a vigorous life and ripened experience to the well-being of the people in the midst of whom the life has been spent. As a rule our town councillors and aldermen are men who through life have satisfied the demand Cromwell made in lieu of his decayed serving men: "Give me men who make some conscience of what they do."

Turning to another aspect of the life of the business man, it will hardly be disputed that his surroundings and duties afford scope for the display and development of moral qualities in a very marked degree. He must for many a juncture and business crisis be a man of courage and resolution. There is often risk, sometimes adventure, and almost always enterprise to call his more daring aptitude into play. There is a constant making towards a goal, a fixed object of endeavour, in which he can find inspiration, and which kindles his

enthusiasm. J. R. Lowell says of General McClellan
that he had many excellent qualities but he lacked
enthusiasm. He had caution but no ardour. Caution
in a business man is one of the most needful qualities,
but no less in the warehouse than on the battle-field
there is need for the head of a firm, of a department or
of an office, to have the power of inspiring to effort
those under his care and direction. He must feel and
be able to make those about him feel that the business
of his department and of the house he represents must
be in the front rank by merit, giving his highest and
best thought to making the opportunities which sometimes disappoint those who wait for them. Business
men must be aggressive; they must be leaders, and
not followers.

That enterprise may be and should be combined
with caution, however, goes without saying. In
business life, as in all other, discretion is the better
part of valour ; indeed, the courage of confidence and
assurance can only be his who acts upon conviction
and well-grounded expectancy. Such associations as
the Manchester Trade Protection Society, and all other
movements to secure a safe trade, only tend to foster
the spirit of enterprise, and to distinguish it from risky
speculation. The Trade Protection Society has for its
membership a number of gentlemen representing the
different branches of the wholesale and retail trade of
Manchester, and its main objects are to make enquiries
as to the status of traders in all parts of the empire
and some parts of Europe, to collect debts for the
members, to wind up insolvent estates, and to watch

legislation in all matters affecting the trades of the district, taking action therein as circumstances seem to warrant; there can be no doubt that the society renders good service to its members.

The business world is ever testing the strength of the more personal moral qualities. No day passes without furnishing its opportunity of connivance with something wrong, until the principles of a man are fully understood and his integrity beyond attack. The man that connives at wrong will in his own character, and not unfrequently in his own circumstances, pay dearly for it. Reliability and trust are based upon integrity, and it is not difficult to see that the upright man stands in a position of command in the keen strife of the commercial life of to-day, the man whose "word is his bond." Scrupulous integrity is strength. "There is no mistake greater," says a writer, "than to suppose the conscience can do a little sin and not suffer ; that little sin is the one weak point." It is the point of insecurity ever afterwards ; it is the very prolific source of more sins.

It should be an axiom amongst all in positions of authority, that no man is fit to command who cannot command himself. Adam Smith says "self-command is not only in itself a great virtue, but from it all other virtues seem to derive their lustre." Retaliation often violates propriety, and leaves a twofold wrong in the place of one: the mistake or wrong of the offender, and the wrong done to oneself by hasty and ungoverned action. It is the vain and the weak man who has little self-control, and who thinks that a bullying manner shows spirit. " It should never be forgotten that we ought to show to those who happen to be placed within our power or who depend on us, forbearance, lenity, and reserve in using their services, and mildness in delivering commands. Each one should feel that he is forbidden to diminish the sum of human happiness, by enforcing unnecessary labour and confinement, or to insult his servants by harsh, scornful, or opprobrious language; nor ought harmless pleasures to be refused; and by the same principle of not diminishing the sum of human happiness, we are forbidden causeless or inconsiderate anger, habitual peevishness, and groundless suspicion."*

There is one other manly quality which business life is specially calculated to foster, and that is honourable emulation without envy or jealousy. Men who, by dint of hard work and continuous effort, have raised themselves to high positions in the world of commerce or in the firm to which they belong, are able to appreciate the like success in others, knowing its cost. Bitter feelings are sometimes engendered by a too-conscious rivalry; but the true state of mind and heart for a successful and happy business-life is quite opposed both to such feelings and to any exhibition of them. There are many opportunities afforded of ruling down such unworthy impulses, and replacing them by manlier and more generous ones. For instance, a competitor's warehouse may be destroyed by fire, leaving him so short of stock that he is unable to

---

* Paley, in his chapter on Moral and Political Philosophy.

discharge pressing orders. Any who has suffered similarly well knows the great inconvenience and difficulty of such circumstances. It is but a simple thing for the heads of a neighbouring warehouse to offer to let their competitor have a little space in their warehouse or any goods that are required for special orders, or boxes, canvas, or any office materials, if they happen to be needed. Amidst all the discords and jealousies of this competitive age, when every man must sometimes feel impelled to join in Wordsworth's invocation to Milton—

> We are selfish men,
> Oh, raise us up, return to us again,
> And give us manners, virtue, freedom, powers,—

it is still possible to remain united and calm in the consciousness of power and rectitude; and the success which has placed others on a high pedestal will only evoke our esteem and minister to the spirit within us of true and noble emulation.

CHAPTER VII.

TO YOUNG MEN.

IN entering the business world, you are entering a school in which the lessons to be learnt are of the most broadening and absorbing character. Its teachings are on finance, law, politics (*i.e.*, the art of governing and administering), geography, specified industries, and, by no means least in importance, human nature. It is a school equally for moral training; men are born to greater aspirations and larger life by its discipline; they learn to bear and to forbear, to be patient under annoyance, to keep down wrath, to look mercifully on a poor, suffering, but honest debtor; to cheer the needy with timely encouragement and help, to inspire the desponding to effort. It is a capital school, if a man is true at heart, and has faith in himself and in a helping God.

Each new generation sees the intellectual life of the business world of a higher order. There is more to be learnt and known; new departments, new developments, new tastes bring with them not only more to be understood and grasped, but are ever introducing fresh problems for solution, the weighing of principle against principle and method against method, demanding the most careful and thoughtful attention. But when once this intelligent zeal is thrown into the various business operations of our city, there will be a restoration of the prestige which has for so many years attached to the name of the Manchester man of business.

A gentleman once remarked to the writer: " I don't see why a young fellow with means should put himself into a warehouse, and be shut up day by day dealing with a lot of nobodies, passing by opportunities· for pleasure and intellectual culture in a better atmosphere and in better society." We grant it would not be difficult to find a more cheerful climate, and if a youth be fond of science, or study of any kind, he may do well by devoting himself to it; yet one would hardly say that the life of the commercial man, conducting a large home and shipping business, is such as to leave his mind uncultivated and unexpanded. He must be acquainted with the raw and manufactured products of almost every country, and must know the time to buy, and the requirements of his own customers in this and other countries before he enters upon his purchases. He has financial and banking arrangements with the various parts of the world to which he exports or from which he imports. He must be familiar with the rates of exchange, government regulations, and custom duties, and with modes of conveyance and freights. He must exercise constant supervision over the bleaching, dyeing, and finishing of goods. He must watch that the trade marks of his firm are not used by unscrupulous or innocent traders, be constantly in contact with men of real power, who have an intelligent grip of their business, and will have, in his capacity of trader, to deal with commodities in so many shapes and forms and in such varied operations. We say it is an honourable and useful life, however regarded ; trade and commerce afford employment to the millions, revenue to the state, develop taste, extend and perfect civilisation, and give that knowledge of the world and of each other that the experience gained is of value in numerous ways amongst one's own countrymen or fellow-citizens.

Excellence is therefore worth attaining ; aim at it. We shall never succeed in what we undertake unless we have high thoughts of its worth, and take pleasure in it. There is one practice or habit amongst youths and young men against which we would speak a word of warning. It is a common remark, and expresses a too common state of feeling: "I don't care; I do as much as my share," or "as much as I am paid for; and if my master will not allow me this or permit that, then I shall not do any more; I shall not trouble about saving him anything in any way." Now, nothing can be more contrary to your interest, from whatever point you view the matter. It is wrong in principle, and hazardous in practice. It is possible that your employer may be thoughtless and ungenerous, or that a fellow-servant may rise in favour by unfair means and beat you in the race ; in either case nothing is gained by you by your assumption of carelessness. You are the loser in forfeiting the satisfaction and enjoyment of having done your duty, of having used every faculty and power you possess in your work. The evidence of a thousand records and the experience of thousands more point to the reward, and prove it to be as certain as anything human that toil and patience will win at last. The old saying is a good one, "Two blacks do not make a white"—they are but two blacks in the end. As a point of honour, as a point of prudence, regard your duty as sacred; discharge to the full extent of your mental and physical powers the work that you have undertaken; it is worth doing well; excellence is worth attaining; and no one ought to expect to reap where he has not sown. In speaking of success and aiming at it, it is well to remember the truth illustrated by Emerson in his *Conduct of Life,* that "Concentration may be made very greatly the source of energy with many. Concentration stops all miscellaneous activity, and directs our force on one or a few points, as the gardener, by severe pruning, forces the sap of the tree into one or two vigorous limbs, instead of suffering it to spindle into a sheaf of twigs . . . the one prudence, therefore, in life is concentration; the one evil, dissipation."

To win success in business, as in everything else, you must be strong as men. The *man* is the *thinker.* Our power to think is our power to know, and "knowledge is power." We must bend to the laws that environ us. Bend to Nature's laws, and she will rejoice your heart; bend to moral laws, and your reward will be greater still. The price must be paid for strength of life and success in it. "Grudge not labour, grudge not pain, sorrow, disappointment, or distress of any kind;—all is for your good if you can endeavour and endure." Better counsel was never given than this of Carlyle's to a young aspirant to literary fame. If success is to be ours, we must win it, and often wrest it from adverse circumstance. The truest life is that which is itself a growth; which grows by pain and learns from disappointment to endeavour and endure. Nothing can be said of a man more hopeful and inspiring than that he is growing; nothing more dispiriting and hopeless than that he has ceased to grow. Whatever our business circumstances, we should see to it that we are growing as men; there is eternal promise in that, and we shall be ready, fortified in spirit and in wisdom, to seize the golden opportunity when it presents itself. There can be no more doubtful commendation of a man than to say he is contented. Rest and content are not for man. Restlessness, *i.e.*, with regard to ourselves and our progress, is divine evidence that we are born for immortality. A growing manhood is not attained by merely furnishing a favourable environment; surroundings minister to it; but the birth and growth of the higher manhood of courage, rectitude, and love go on within the man. Grow yourself, and your circumstances will grow with you; if they do not, *you* are not the less; if your circumstances grow and you do not, you will present an anomaly comparable to the state of manhood's "sixth age," whose "hose" are "a world too wide for his shrunk shank."

All men need recreation, but none so much as youths and young men; your physical frame and mental powers are growing, and both must have exercise for their healthy development. If your work is manual, you need mental recreation; if your work is mental, you need physical recreation. Manly pastimes are to be found of both kinds. Amongst the former are chess and some games with cards; amongst the latter, such outdoor sports as cricket, football, lacrosse, cycling, and the gymnasium. Early manhood requires the moral aid of absorbing pastimes, especially such as give vent to the animal spirits of youth, and help to subdue its passions.

Let us put to you concisely and frankly what we desire to advise:—

I. Young men should find one or more smart, manly young fellows with whom to associate for purposes of society and recreation. Above all, be judicious in your choice of a girl companion; a good wife is the highest prize a man can win; but do not be led away by the fascinations of a dressy, giddy girl, who has no backbone of character. Such a one will soon cease to be a companion; you would then crave and seek other society; habits of drinking and gambling and worse often ensue; and we have seen again and again manly and honourable young men fall step by step, until at last they stand before the magistrate for disorderly conduct or neglect of home. Noble friendships strengthen the heart in virtue, *i.e.*, in valour or manliness; evil friendships corrupt the soul.

II. Find time to read useful and good books; make companions of them. They will be an unfailing source of strength to you in any position of life you may be called to occupy.

III. Be scrupulous in all points of honour. Never do a girl a wrong, nor trifle with her affections; be

J

true and loyal in friendship; honourable in all your
service, industrious and truthfuL   In business, be accurate in your statements, do not exaggerate with regard
to anything you may have to sell. We have always said
that a man who tells a lie is wanting in brain power ;
if he cannot conduct a case in court, transact business
in the office, or sell goods at the counter without telling
falsehoods, he is not possessed of the qualifications
needful for the position he holds ; there should be no
dallying with the question of truth.   To resort to
falsehood is to make a confession of weakness.   Take
the case of a young man of moderately good education,
who does not read a good solid book in twelve months,
and who consequently is doing little to mature his
mind, widen his judgment, and increase his knowledge of men and things. He is placed by the side of a
well-educated young fellow who is constantly developing his intellectual powers. The latter carries through
his work with success and confidence; the former,
however, is conscious of comparative failure; he is
anxious to be the equal of the man of trained mind,
and resorts to lying and deceit, making the excuse that
he is driven to it in order to do his trade and maintain
his position.   The fact is, and it is a fact which will
sooner or later be manifest, that he is wanting in
capacity or administrative ability, and he is left behind
in the race not only by the man who, like himself, had
the advantage of education, but by the man who has not
many words in his vocabulary, and who is painfully conscious of the want of early education, yet who is so
sterling in character and so reliable in every way that

he commands the admiration of his customers and of his employers and wins for himself a good position. Of course, where education and ability are combined with manly integrity, the man possessing all these qualities rises to the highest position ; but it is wisdom for every man, whatever his capabilities and advantages, to be strictly truthful and honest, remembering that honesty includes punctuality, faithful service, and the use only of one's own and not of another man's goods or time, and that truthfulness means saying what is strictly correct, and in the clearest language you can command. The advice said to have been given by an Oldham man to a friend will bear repetition: "I have tried both sorts, but I have found out that honesty is the best policy." Do not test the principle as he did; but we sincerely wish you would accept the testimony of thousands who have arrived at the same conclusion.

IV. Do not be carried away by false ambition. There is a weak ambition, founded on conceit, which greatly ensnares some young men. Many are exceedingly anxious to be thought something they are not; they ape their superiors in habit and style of living. From our own observation and frequent conversations with men of experience, we have learned that disaster often arises from this source. A young man gets into a warehouse or office, and, after being there a few years, is receiving a salary of, say, £120 per annum. He is acquainted with another young man in the same house, perhaps a year or two his junior, receiving, it may be, £150 per annum. He feels himself quite the latter's equal, possibly is so, and could have filled the

better position quite as ably if it had been his good
fortune to secure it. He is quite as popular in the club,
in the cricket or football field, and he is desirous to
appear just as well as the other; so he must pay to
this and subscribe to that, live in as good apartments,
smoke the same cigars, undergoing all the expenses
with his income of £120 which cost the other nearly
the whole of his £150. Instead of studying the rule
of three to find out what must be the result, he only
studies the rule of two, viz., his wants and the source
from which they are to be supplied. He is not long
before he finds a source of supply in trifling thefts.
His master will not voluntarily give him more money;
he cannot borrow, and we believe it is often under a
sense of disappointment, and the feeling that he has a
right to larger remuneration, that the first robberies are
committed. He grows in boldness as he remains for
a time undiscovered, only to wake up to the discovery
that there is a rule of three, the third factor being the
apportionment of justice by the magistrate. Have
patience and wait. Keep company with young men of
intelligence and character, whose pleasure is in reasonable and inexpensive recreation. By all means seek
recreation; take part in athletic games, which will help
to make better men of you in every sense; but live
within your position and means. Don't ape the great,
but aim at it; and, if you have brain power, tact, and
energy, you will reach your goal. It would be well if
every young man in this city would honestly consider
his position. If you are the son of a merchant or professional man, and have the capacity of your father, do

you labour as he laboured? Do you give the time and attention, and bestow the amount of thought upon your calling that he has done? If so, your future is secure. But if you have less ability, are morose, wanting in urbanity, are given to tall talk, and give three or four hours a day to your duties where your father gave ten, then the result will be the want of success, which it is fair and just to expect. There are always about you industrious, aspiring young men, fired by a worthy ambition to excel, who are capable of stepping into your place. You have the start of them, and if you avail yourselves of it you will retain the lead and win the regard of all; but if you throw the position away, do not blame your successor, the fault is your own.

The only safe course is to accept cheerfully your present position, and determine that you will only move out of it by dint of industry and application. Happiness is the lot of the man who lives within his income and manfully accepts his position in life, seeking to improve himself that he may be ready for the day of greater things. There are thousands of men in this city, earning from twenty-five to fifty shillings a week, who have more real domestic and personal enjoyment, who are more respected and have a higher reputation amongst their equals and amongst men in higher stations than themselves, than the thousands who receive larger incomes and make the spendthrift's use of them. We do not say, of course, that poverty is a blessing, but integrity and moderation are. He has not touched the first rung of the ladder which leads to an honourable position and to a strong and manly life, who speaks of his fellow-salesman or clerk as a member of the goody-goody class because he prefers to go to a lecture or to class-work, instead of to the club to play billiards or to the theatre or hotel for the evening.

V. There is a pride which is a serious hindrance to many youths. Fresh from successes at school or indulgence at home, they think their capacity is considerably above the average, and that they should not be called upon to do any work that seems drudgery to them. Now, this drudgery is part of the training for business life, and an essential part. Nobody can fill the higher positions well who has not learned to fill the lower. He cannot understand with the same clearness how the work of the subordinates should be done, nor can he confer on them the benefit of raising them to great proficiency.

The same kind of pride impels some to seek positions for which they are totally unqualified. One would not stifle any true, energetic purpose; but many young men do seriously miss their calling, and fall into grievous troubles, in which unfortunately others are often involved. It is a mark of instability and must end in ruinous consequences for a youth to decline to take the advice of those who have experienced the arduousness of life, and seen the inevitable fate of vain, incompetent men.

A true magnanimity can only grow up in the modest, self-contained man. To over-rate oneself and under-rate one's fellow-worker greatly mars a life, and it is a source of blindness as to elements of weakness in oneself and strength in others. The failure to see another's merit is blindness to merit; failure to recognise one's own defects is one of its most baneful results.

VI. Allow us now to indicate one or two of the dangers which arise from the temptations besetting the lives of the young men of to-day. We refer to smoking, drinking, and gambling. All young people should abstain from intoxicating drinks and from tobacco, at least until they are matured both in physical powers and in judgment—say, till they are twenty-three or twenty-four; after that period everyone should be able to exercise restraint over himself, and probably will be able if untainted by early habit. We have not the slightest desire to dictate, being in no sense a fanatic, and having no wish to curtail young men's legitimate pleasures; but to our certain knowledge many young men indulge in these habits who cannot afford to do so, and who have to deny themselves the means of education, decent clothing, and in some cases even proper food. These habits often lead on to other modes of expenditure quite inimical to their interests, and many have confessed to us that they have started on a downward path by smoking and just taking a glass with a friend. Again and again we pass in the streets the wrecks of once respectable young people whom we have known in business.

The following figures are very striking, showing the number of years men of given ages are expected to live according as they are temperate or intemperate:—

Years of age.	Temperate.	Intemperate.
20	44	15
30	36	13
40	28	11
50	21	10
60	14	6

A question on which we feel very strongly is that of gambling and its increasing prevalence.* Again, the writer would say, in order that he be not misunderstood, that he believes in the necessity for amusement and exercise as a means of recreation for young people. It has come under our observation for some years that a good athlete generally turns out a good man in whatever calling; and one of our medical men once said, " Let us see what sort of hips and thighs a lad has, never mind his head; I want to see physical power." It is no less true that the young of both sexes need games for their employment during winter evenings; some prefer billiards, others chess, others dice, dominoes, draughts, or cards. One can have no objection to these as games, but there is much that is to be condemned in playing for money. Why the first question, when a game is decided upon, should be, "What shall we play for ?" and why the remark should be so often heard, "I cannot play well unless I have something at stake," we cannot understand. It is simply a habit, and one that often leads to great mischief. We regard gambling in every form as unmanly, unreasonable, and ungodly. We regard gambling as

---

* See also Jottings, article reprinted from *City News.*

unmanly, because it is necessarily enfeebling in its effects upon the will. " The man who ' has a bet on ' is, in many cases, a purely passive spectator of the rise and fall of his fortunes, so soon as ever his bet is made. Unless he descend to dishonourable practices—a possibility too mean to be now entered into—he has nothing to do but to await the issue and accept it. Nothing can be more enfeebling to the will than this self-imposed passivity. The man is teaching himself to depend on luck, whereas the active pursuit of ends, whether by plodding or pushing, is the mark of the energetic will. A strong man always has a strong hand in the determining of his own fortunes. A distinction holds in some sense between games of skill for chance and mere speculation, but in so far as gambling leads men away from the paths of labour which support themselves, minister to their strength of character and serve others, the practice is unmanly."

Betting on horses is the most serious form of gambling that comes under our observation. We have seen and heard so much of this practice and its effects, that our horror of it exceeds anything that we can express in words. If we could reach the eye, or ear, or the understanding of the young men of this city, we would earnestly appeal to them to avoid it ; the way of the gambler is bestrewn with sorrow and anxiety, and generally ends in great distress to himself and family. We could give numerous instances of a most painful character where young men, feeling themselves bound by this so-called "debt of honour," have robbed their employers, lost character and situation, and blasted the proud hopes of good parents. We know there are some men who indulge in the practice in a small and comparatively innocent form and get no particular harm, but these are the exceptions; and the great fact holds that we have no right to get another person's money without giving the *quid pro quo* in some shape, and the cultivation of the habit leads in numberless cases to ruin. This in itself proves the unreasonableness of the practice; but the very basis of gambling, and especially of betting, is an irrational one, and this because profit is made, when it is made, not out of knowledge but out of ignorance. In all rational pursuit of wealth the chances for all increase as the knowledge of all widens. Though the capitalist and labouring classes are often regarded and spoken of as competing the one against the other for their share of the produce of industry, it is none the less true that each is richer by the other's knowledge. The wider the information of the master, the keener his foresight, and the surer his grasp of manufacturing and commercial principles, the better captained and the better paid his men. The more thorough the education, both general and technical, and the greater the knowledge and mental powers of the employé, the higher is his value to his master. In every rational and healthy pursuit of wealth, the knowledge of one becomes the benefit of all. In gambling, the reverse is the case. Ignorance is capitalised. What the bookmaker or private betting man depends upon is not the knowledge, but the ignorance of his client or victim, as one may prefer to call him. Of course, there are two parties to a bet, each willingly entering into it ; and the same is true of either party, each is hoping to profit by the other's ignorance. The fact that most bets take the form of "odds against," offered and taken, shows that a certain quantity of ignorance in one mind is being pitted against an equal, less a greater quantity of ignorance in another mind. Ben Brierley, writing in the *Manchester Guardian* upon "gradely folk," gives a definition of "lump-yeads." This "term," he says, "was wont to be applied to young bar-parlour men who read nothing but sporting papers, who pretended to know everything, but knew nothing except how to silence modest intelligence by the offer of a bet." The term "lump-yead," coupled with the definition of it, shows that Ben Brierley regards the practice as irrational.

Certainly the practice is ungodly, for it is intensely selfish. The winner only profits by another's loss. If life seems slow, look around you, and, in addition to many healthy modes of physical enjoyment, you will find opportunity for the exercise of your mental powers, and perchance in some such noble form as the help of your fellows, instead of ministering to their ruin. Learn, at least, to possess yourselves in patience. Do not seek another's wealth. Toil manfully for your living, and endeavour to improve your circumstances. Hold yourselves independent of pity, by being men of will and not creatures of chance. Command respect by the creation of wealth rather than the wresting it from another.

We only speak of young men's dangers in order, if possible, to awaken your desires for a true and worthy life. We would create an enthusiasm for great and good things. Each man that is true in all his dealings, magnanimous and unselfish, is a power for good amongst his fellows. "A man," said Isaiah, "shall be as the shadow of a great rock in a weary land." And any man who yields to the better impulses within him may live nobly, doing his part in the world's uplifting.

> No life
> Can be pure in its purpose and strong in its strife,
> And all life not be purer and stronger thereby.

Some time ago a gentleman called at a large house in this city, asking if he could be supplied with goods and could have credit for a certain amount, on the usual trade terms, stating he was in business in such a city, in a country far away across the waters which it takes weeks to reach. Questions were put to him as to his family connections, early training and experience, financial position, and the reasons why he had left his native land and adopted the place in which he now resides. He replied, " This is rather a new experience you are putting me through, but it will afford me pleasure to answer all your enquiries, and will give you a short narrative of my life, especially that part which has been gone through since I left England. Not succeeding in this country as one would desire, the ground being too well covered and occupied by intelligent, pushing young men, who were, like myself, anxious to make a position. I had served my time to the dry goods trade, and felt competent to take a responsible situation. Finding the way difficult here, I

resolved to try my fortune on another shore. After
casting about and making enquiries, I decided that the
country where my business is now conducted was, on
the whole, the best I could select. I bade adieu to my
family and friends and crossed the ocean, landing at a
large seaport town. Was in good health, had a little
money in my pocket, possessing fair average abilities
for the business in which I had so far been engaged,
called upon the various wholesale and retail dealers,
offering my services at a moderate salary. Weeks
passed by and no probability appeared of finding occupation; whatever report was given of my experience,
however low the salary offered to be accepted, all
seemed in vain. My patience was severely tried; my
funds were getting smaller, but I was determined not to
return home. I started out one morning resolute upon
finding something, even if it was carrying coals or wheel-
ing a barrow. Had not been out long before observing
in a window a paper, on which was written 'A bottler
wanted.' Entered the office and asked what was the
kind of work a bottler had to perform. The reply was
prompt and decisive, 'Bottling ale.' 'Can I see the work,
sir?' Reply: 'Yes, if you open the door before you.'
Opening the door, saw a number of men and youths all
vigorously engaged bottling ale. Then immediately returned to the office, and said to the gentleman, 'I have
seen the work. What are the wages?' He replied,
'Twenty-four shillings per week.' I expressed my
willingness to accept the situation, feeling sure I could
do it well, after a day's practice. An engagement was
made, and for some months I diligently followed my

new occupation. One day a junior was larking, and threw a half-pint bottle at another youth. It missed him and passed through the window. It was soon arranged that the square must be replaced. A plumber was sent for, and I watched the operation of taking out the remaining part of the old glass and the putting in of the new square. When it was done, enquired of the man what he would charge. He named the price, and I then asked what was the cost of the diamond with which he cut the glass. He told me, and also the cost of the glass and putty. The profit seemed to me very large. It was quite clear, if a fair amount of work could be found, it was a vastly better paying business than bottling ale. Having thought this over a few days, I called upon a large plumber and got all particulars as to the cost of the glass, putty, diamond, &c., which would be required to start a man in a small way. After a good many experiments, became confident I could do the work satisfactorily, and having money enough in my possession to enable me to make the start, I left my situation, determining to leave the coast and work up country, calling upon shopkeepers, at private houses, and farmhouses, putting in squares, where they had broken ones, at a moderate price. My stock was soon used up, and had to be replenished on a rather larger scale. Did this again and again, until I found myself a little better off. Then thought if I could find a decent town where there was room for a new trader, it would be well to see if I could not make a start in business premises of my own instead of tramping the country. Shortly after that met with a place which seemed everything I could desire. Returned to the city, stated to a large wholesale store what I had seen, named the extent of my capital, and asked if they would supply me with sufficient goods to open the store, on which they could have any security they liked, and I would see them with full particulars at fixed times, and felt sure they would find me a good customer. The proposal was considered. In due time I was allowed to select the necessary stock, and I returned to my new home, which was to be my centre of action for the future. Then opened the store, and succeeded in winning the confidence of the people in and around the town. I gradually extended the size of the store, increased the quantity and variety of goods, and now I am free from all liability; have a large, general stock; and (taking a book out of his breast pocket) now have that amount to my credit, in my bankers' hands, viz., £10,000, which I should like you to get confirmed by writing to my bankers, or their agents in London." The statement as to capital and character was fully confirmed. To the mind of the present writer this is an interesting record of what can be accomplished by a man who is resolute in working his own way and fighting his own battle in life.

CHAPTER VIII.

PERSONAL REMINISCENCES.

THE year 1854 was a memorable one in the history of the firm of Rylands and Sons. On the evening of the first of March, a fire broke out in the grey department of their warehouse. The origin of the fire was always thought to be the throwing of a lighted match into the grid, which ignited some straw lying in the area of the window. This is the most probable explanation; the use of straw in packing was very common at that time, and, no doubt, a considerable quantity would accumulate in any quiet corner whither it might be blown.

The fire spread rapidly; and the writer, knowing the position of the books, rushed in at the front door, and was making his way towards the office, when a powerful hand grasped his arm. He turned and saw that it was a fireman. In a voice that he still remembers, he said, " Who are you, and where are you going ? " " To the office, to get out some books." " Go back," he said, " or your life will be lost." " But," said the writer, " I know where to place my hand on important books." " I don't care what the —— you know; go out." And he showed the way out somewhat unceremoniously.

By the time the street was reached, however, the fire had burst into the office, and in another minute all was in flames.

Now came the anxious moment. What would become of the safe containing all the ledgers, in which the firm's accounts were kept, as well as a considerable amount of money in notes and gold? We watched that safe with an interest and anxiety not to be described. The stock was so far consumed as to leave only salvage, and, if the books were also lost, what *would* be the result? Fortunately, the safe resisted the flames, though in the centre of a furnace of fire for hours; and the firm was able to trace all its accounts.

In spite of this serious disaster and the keen temporary discouragement which it naturally caused the chief of the firm, the business was resumed in other premises during the rebuilding, and the year's turnover was larger than that of any previous year, showing the truth of Seneca's maxim, "We are sure to get the better of fortune if we but grapple with her."

A little before the fire an accident happened, which impressed itself upon the writer's memory by the associated facts and the remarkable escape of Mr. William Rylands. Four storeys fell in at the Tib Street end of the warehouse, the stairs from the pattern-card room snapping in two. Mr. William Rylands was just leaving the room, and had actually taken one step down the stairs, when they fell away, leaving only the step on which he was standing, literally confirming the scriptural statement, " There is

K

but one step between us and death." With his usual
calm manner he turned round without a word or
ejaculation of any kind; got on to the floor of the
room he had just left, and crept quietly along to an
opening in the roof. Mr. Rylands soon began to enquire for his son. Several had seen him go up the
stairs, but none had noticed his return. We called out
for him in all directions, but no answer came; and the
father quite broke down, being convinced he had
perished in the ruins. Meanwhile, Mr. William had
made his way along the roof, and, having entered
another part of the warehouse, was returning to where
he knew his father would be awaiting him. A short
but interesting account of Mr. William Rylands was
given in the *Manchester City News*, April, 1865, in one
of a series of papers on "The principal Manchester
firms: their rise and progress."

About the year 1844, the late Mr. William Rylands,
second son of the gentleman who has so long been the
sole principal of the firm, left school, being then about
eighteen years of age. As, however, his health was
constitutionally frail, his father arranged that his son
should travel, accompanied by a tutor, with the twofold
object of extending his knowledge of the world, and
recruiting his health and strength.

About 1852 or 1853, he was well enough to attend
to business at New High Street, and he took part in
the general management of the concern. He was
amiable, of genial manners, of a generous and noble
disposition; with great talent and aptitude for business
or for anything else that he undertook; very quiet,

unpretending, yet very far-seeing, and devotedly fond of literary and scientific pursuits and mental culture. Naturally very ardent and enthusiastic in all he undertook, his health was constantly giving way, and his father's earnest desire was that he should relax from business and again travel.

After having for some years acted as partner, and taken a very efficient share in the general management, it was arranged that he should go up the Mediterranean, and travel through Egypt, Syria, &c., in order to try the effects of a warmer climate. He was, however, suddenly taken ill before this journey could be undertaken, and so rapidly did his disease gain upon his weakly constitution that it baffled all the skill and unceasing attention of his medical men. He was prematurely cut down in the thirty-third year of his age. He was beloved and much lamented by all who knew him. Deep, almost inconsolable, was his father's grief; for he had reckoned on his being not only his own solace and stay in the evening of life, but also that he would be, by his virtues, talents, and property, a great blessing to others, especially to his native city, Manchester, and thus perpetuate the name of Rylands with honour to future generations.

Happily the accident, which suggested this reference to Mr. William Rylands, ended without injury to any one. A large number of men were at work on all of the floors, which so suddenly collapsed, a few minutes before; but by doorways leading into the part of the building still undisturbed and other outlets all escaped unhurt.

The writer has the liveliest recollection of the Fenian excitement in 1867, when Allen, Larkin, and O'Brien were hung at the New Bailey, where the Lancashire and Yorkshire Railway goods station now stands. Intense excitement prevailed throughout the town: the attack on the police van, the murder of the officer Brett, the savage treatment of all in charge of the van, and the battering the van itself underwent, were all of a character to cause apprehension, and in the minds of many people created consternation in a degree approaching panic. The day of the execution was miserably damp and foggy. When the poor fellows had suffered the extreme penalty of the law, the threats of vengeance caused many to fear very troublous times for the town. Amongst others, our firm received a private letter advising us that on a certain night it was intended to make an attack upon our warehouse. Accordingly, we called a band of young men together to form themselves into a company, and, with appointed leaders, we undertook to watch, ready for whatever duty might lie before us. The warehouse was closed at the usual time and in the usual way. An informal meeting was held amongst those who stayed behind to meet the expected attack. The points where protection would be most needed were decided upon, and we divided off, some taking up their position on either side of New High Street, others in Bread Street. Early in the morning we saw a considerable number of Irish coming up Market Street. One of the policemen outside, with whom we were in communication, gave us the hint to be prepared for anything that might arise. It proved, however, to be a false alarm. They were simply a number of harvest-men going from the Victoria to the London Road Station. In a few minutes they had all passed, and the streets were quiet again, except for the footstep of an occasional policeman or of some poor creature pacing the streets in loneliness and want. In about an hour after this we heard footsteps again. We could tell from the sound that they were passing up the side streets. We looked for an officer, but none was to be seen. Presently, one of our company ran across New High Street to inform the others that mischief was brewing in the hovel and in Bridgewater Place. We went immediately to the door of the hovel, walking in our stockings to avoid making the slightest noise, and two or three of us lay down on the floor, near the door in the Bread Street warehouse, to listen. We heard a number of footsteps, and shortly we heard, "Are you nearly ready?" and the reply came from somewhere very close to where we were, "James, hold this." "All right!" "George, mind what you are doing." "All right! say when you are ready." "Yes." It was in the still dead of night; we had had no sleep; our minds had been in a state of the utmost tension for the last four or five hours; every footstep was exciting; every word of the deepest interest, as its import might be that the very next moment the door at which we were listening and the adjoining windows would be broken in, and a set of ruffians upon us more than our equals in number and strength. We rose to our feet, put on our boots, took our weapons, ourselves threw open the door, and shouted, as though we had a thousand strong men behind us, demanding their business there. To our no small relief, we found that the voices and footsteps were those of a number of policemen, who had made a rendezvous of the hovel, and a table of our door ledge; and the expressions we had overheard and which had been to us so pregnant with meaning had reference only to their preparations for a light meal. After this, we fastened up the place again, had a little all-round enjoyment and refreshment, and then retired in the full belief that all was safe, and that no mischief would befall us or the house.

RECOLLECTIONS OF MR. ALDERMAN GEORGE BOOTH AND MR. JOHN WADE.

We have a very vivid recollection of the day Mr. Booth left the firm of Rylands and Sons to commence business on his own account. Having sat by his side at the desk, and been actively engaged as teacher in a Sunday school where he was superintendent, we had become much attached to him, and felt the wrench of his removal intensely. Alderman Booth was a man of strict integrity, very punctual in his attention to any duty that he undertook, and in every way most reliable and faithful. In his records, whether of figures or facts, he was most accurate; nothing irritated him so much as an error in any book or account, whether as to money received on his occasional journeys or at the counter in the office. He was almost invariably correct. Industry, indefatigable labour, was his great characteristic; when he once realised his duty no pains were spared, no time was begrudged in the accomplishment of the purpose before him; he was great in detail; everything must be followed to its utmost limit; in fact, the love of detail was his to a weakness, for he spent time and ability in small things which should have been devoted to matters of greater importance affecting the growth of the concern in which he was occupying an important position. He was a generous, kind-hearted, intelligent man, worthy of the affectionate regard in which he was held by those who associated with him in life.

We remember one Saturday afternoon he invited twelve young men, including myself, to a walking tour over the Glossop hills. When we had climbed to the top, a gamekeeper came up, and was going to take all of us into custody, "on account of the damage we were doing and the many birds we had killed," as he said. We tried to pacify him by saying we had no desire to do any mischief, and would act exactly as he told us, but the more we assured him of our sorrow for any harm we might unintentionally have done, and our desire to avoid any further wrong, the more violent and offensive he became. At last, five or six of us surrounded him, and said, "We have acted as kindly as we could and expressed our regret at what you say has occurred, and if you continue to use such disgraceful language, we have no alternative but to give you a downright good thrashing, and leave you on the moor to meditate on the fruits of ungenerous and unmanly treatment. Tell us at once your decision," and we all looked and felt what we said. Happily for us, the man gave way, became gentle as a lamb, and spent a considerable time in showing us nests and eggs, contributing in no small degree to make what at one moment promised to be an unpleasant afternoon into a very enjoyable one.

Alderman Booth delighted in giving a pleasant surprise. On one occasion, he invited us to join him, his brother, Mr. Hugh Booth, and a ministerial friend of his, in a ramble round the waterworks in Longdendale, in which, it is well known, he took an active interest, and a very enjoyable walk we had. Just at five o'clock, the surprise he had prepared, of which he had not given us the slightest hint, came most agreeably upon us. He took us into the garden of an old friend of his, where we found he had arranged beforehand a most sumptuous dinner-tea should be ready. He had a warm, generous heart, and it delighted him to give a little treat in that fashion.

If Alderman Booth had married a good intelligent lady, he would have developed into a larger and broader man, in many respects. Had he enjoyed

> That rare communion, which links
> With what woman feels purely, what man nobly thinks,
> And, by hallowing life's hopes, enlarges life's strength,

he would doubtless have become a greater power in his adopted city, where he was always kind, genial, and helpful to the aged and sorrowful, and a guide and friend to many young men.

Much more might be said about his career as a business man and Christian worker, but we will content ourselves with referring to one pleasant evening spent at Ashley Lane, the scene of his more than fifty years' labour. We were invited to be present at a meeting of all the old teachers and scholars, when a testimonial was to be presented to Mr. Booth, in the shape of a portrait of himself in oils, executed by Mr. Perkins, the artist who painted the one now hanging in the Town Hall. We were asked to perform the ceremony of unveiling. Speeches were arranged to be delivered by friends, who had known him for many years, some of them acquaintances of more than fifty years' standing. At a given time the veil was withdrawn; it was a moment of joy to all present, and utter amazement to the worthy alderman himself, for the subscriptions had been collected, and the first portrait copied, without his having the least idea of the fact. The evening was a very pleasant one to all, and a very real pleasure to myself, who felt a sincere attachment to the old gentleman, from whom ourself received many kindnesses, and much judicious advice in early life.

We felt then that it is no small or trivial matter for a man to enjoy the consciousness, when life is drawing towards its close, of having cherished desires and patiently laboured for good, and a knowledge that honour clings to his name. Alderman Booth generously devoted much of his time and energy to work of various kinds for the good of others, and always did cheerfully whatever he undertook.

Amongst the many remarkable men we have met, during my sojourn in this city, was a Mr. Wade. His first entry into Manchester was made as a drover, bringing a number of cattle from Yorkshire to a butcher in this city. Something in his manner arrested the attention of the butcher, who said to him, as he was about to return, "Young man, have you engaged to go back immediately?" "No, sir, I am in no hurry," was the reply. "Well, then, stop here a few days; I am in need of a helper, and have work to do for which I think you are well fitted."

He remained, and did his work so well that at the close of the first week his master said to him, "I see you will suit me, and should like you to stay awhile. I will give you so much wages." The offer was accepted and the work entered upon at once. During the first week, the master spoke to his new employé about his interest as a Sabbath school scholar, and said, "I see you are a steady young man, and I should like you to go to the chapel we attend and also to the Sunday school, in which my daughter and I take a deep interest."

John Wade replied, "I am sorry to say I can neither read nor write."

"Never mind, you can go to the young men's class, and you will find the teacher a very kind and agreeable man."

He consented; but on entering the school the superintendent, seeing he was a fine, manly fellow (he stood five feet ten or eleven inches, and was well built), at once asked him to take charge of a class, of which the teacher was unavoidably absent that afternoon. This was more than the young man had expected.

" Oh," said he, " you must excuse me, I am not used to teaching."

" Never mind, you will easily manage a lot of nice little fellows like these."

The young man was too proud to expose his ignorance, and determined to try and do his best. He would watch the next teacher's movements, and, as far as possible, would copy them; besides, he remembered that his master had explained to him how the class in which he was to have been placed was conducted, so he sat down among the boys. One of the lads remarked, " Our teacher is going through the gospel of St. John, and we are at such a chapter;" and they all turned at once to the place. Meantime, John had opened his testament, but unfortunately at the wrong part, which the nearest lad saw in a moment, and called attention to the fact. " Yes, yes," he said, " you are younger than I, I will take your book." The exchange was made, and they began to read. The third boy stumbled at a word and looked to the teacher for assistance. Without exhibiting for a moment his incapacity, he at once realised his position, and turning to the fourth boy said, in a cheerful voice, " Now, my lad, always be ready to help your neighbour." By adopting this plan the whole of the chapter was safely got through, but not in much comfort on John's part. Every moment he had been growing hotter, a fact which became plainly visible in his face; his discomfort being, no doubt, intensified by the unusual confinement in a well-filled room, and by his attire, so very different from that to which he was accustomed. Part of this had been provided for him from his master's wardrobe, and part bought at a second-hand clothes shop. In spite of his misery, however, John tried to follow the example of the teachers round him, and talked to the boys until the bell rang and teaching ceased. An address was then delivered, after which the school closed, very much to the joy of the new teacher, who had more than once promised himself, " no one should catch him there again."

Being questioned on his return as to his success, he told them his experience, and the torture he had gone through, adding, " I shall never be caught in that position again; I will go to the chapel, but no more school for me, thank you; at any rate, not at present." " Oh, don't say so," returned the master; " I will tell you what we can do. We shall know the chapter to be read in the young men's class, and we will read it over every morning and night this week; when I cannot afford the time, my daughter shall read it with you, and explain as much as possible. In a week you will have nearly learned it by heart, and know it quite well enough, at any rate, to take your place in the class. Do, I beg, go again; if not in a week, say, in a fortnight." The latter was promised, the effort was made, and he acquired sufficient confidence to continue. The reading and explanation at home went on for some time, the progress being so marked that he was soon able to render considerable help, both at the chapel and as a teacher in the school, to both of which he gave generously out of his earnings. Meantime, his manifest business ability had secured the warmest approval of the master and his wife. It was soon discovered by the former that the teaching and reading of his daughter were more appreciated than his own, and that she, on her part, never found the time devoted to it too long or the task inconvenient, but was always ready each evening to give the required assistance. So one day John called his employer aside, and said that "his daughter Sarah had not only been very successful in giving him lessons for the school, but had also, at the same time, won his affections, and they had mutually agreed that, with her father's and mother's approval, they should be married." After due consideration, the consent was given, and the two were very soon united. They had not been married long before John saw that his father-in-law was in difficulties. He could not, as in days gone by, go into the market, and buy, paying ready money for his cattle. Being questioned on the matter, he disclosed to his son-in-law the fact of his insolvency. John replied, " Don't say a word to any one. I have saved £120 since entering your service, and that, if properly managed, will be quite sufficient to restore your position in the market. I will take charge of the business, only give me your confidence, let me take my own way, and we will soon put all right again." This was agreed upon, and then John, whom in future we must call Mr. Wade, went to his wife, told her what had passed, and said, " Now, we must for a few years exercise the strictest economy. What do you think we

can manage the house upon, to cover all expenses,
except rent and rates?" She thought the matter over
carefully and named an amount. "Very well," he said,
"you shall have that sum weekly." Mr. Wade continued perseveringly and energetically to push the
business, which increased every year, and the father
lived to see and enjoy not only the old position of
financial ease and comfort, but to see his son-in-law
accumulating a fortune. During these few years, the
thrifty young wife, who had all along silently borne
the grief, which a true child was sure to feel at the
reverse of fortune which had overtaken her parents,
had been saving every shilling she could, until she had
accumulated £120. One morning she came into the
sitting-room, saying, "John, see!" at the same time
pouring out of a bag £120 in gold, with the remark,
" I have saved this out of the money you have given
me for housekeeping; this pays my father's debt, does
it not?" He looked at her, but his heart was too full
to speak. Years after, when he was advanced in life,
the strong man wept as he related this to me. On
Sunday, he and his wife and servant always went to
chapel, locking up the house. Having money always
on the premises, he felt it was his duty to give any
person, who might break in, as much trouble as possible
to find it. Therefore, every Saturday night, he put the
notes and loose cash in a bag, one week placing this
under a mattress, the next in a wardrobe, so varying
its hiding-place every time. On one occasion he
thought he would conceal it under the fireplace, as far
back as possible. It so happened, that particular

evening, there was an extra service at chapel, to which
Mr. and Mrs. Wade remained, the latter telling the
servant to go home and light a fire in the sitting-room,
as it was rather cold. She did so. On their return,
Mr. Wade at once caught sight of the fire, and, remembering the money, he rushed to the grate, and dragged
from beneath the still unburnt bag, all safe. Shortly
after this, to his great sorrow, his beloved wife was
prostrated with a severe and fatal illness. After her
death he retired from business, investing his capital in
various ways, including house and shop property. He
made his will, appointing several well-known gentlemen in the city as executors, and, having no children
of his own, left his property, which was very considerable, to various charities and educational institutions.
Shortly after he sent for me, and expressed his extreme
annoyance at the treatment he had received from a
gentleman connected with one of these institutions,
who ought not to have been guilty of such indiscretions
as were repeated to me. The result was, the first will
was destroyed, and another made, leaving the property
to a large number of nephews and nieces, many of
whom he had never seen.

Though uncultured, not having had the blessing of a
good education and training, such as many have, he
was, nevertheless, as fine in spirit and purpose as in
personal appearance, and though in common with all
human beings he had faults, he had many high qualities. He was keen, shrewd, and far seeing, yet at the
same time generous and helpful to many. Mr. Wade
had one peculiarity, he would never have recourse to

legal measures; if his debtors would not pay without the intervention of the law, the accounts remained unpaid. From the day he entered Manchester, without a decent coat or pair of shoes, to the time of his death, when he was in comparatively affluent circumstances, we never heard of his owing any man a debt. He would keep no books, his business was a cash one, and whatever advantages could be secured by cash payments he was always prepared to take. His career was in many respects a pattern. Would that we had more young men like him! Where now are those who would be found willing to endure the ordeal he passed through in his early Sunday school labours? He was a hero in his position, putting pride completely aside, when by so doing he could secure the improvement of his mind and the good of others. One cannot but admire his action, when his father-in-law's position became known to him, in laying down his hard-earned money, and resolutely determining by his own efforts to maintain the family honour, and return in no stinted form the kindness the old gentleman had shown him, when he was a poor and comparatively destitute lad; nay, the very opportunity, as he told me, gave him great delight. We would not conclude without one further word of praise for his thrifty wife, who with pardonable pride desired to save her father's good name by paying his debt out of her own careful savings, the result of frugal management.

SOME NOTABLE EVENTS.

Amongst the incidents in the writer's Manchester experience indelibly impressed upon his memory stands out the great gala day, October 10th, 1851, in celebration of the Royal visit to the city. The unusualness of the event may be gathered from the following paragraph by Mr. Thomas Nicholson: "If we calculate the eccentricity of the orbit in which Royalty moves by the period that has elapsed since the last visit, and then determine the period of the next visit, it will be close upon the twenty-second century ere the phenomenon is again observed in the streets of Manchester. We wonder what reign that will be in, what kind of people will fill our places to come and see it, who will be mayor; and, though last not least, whether the town council will uniformly agree to wear gowns on that occasion?"

Mr. Procter indicates the special interest excited by the visit. "From the orchards and meadow lands," he says, "came plenty of rosy cheeks to mingle during one day with the lily features of the city. Even the Infirmary, house of accident, amputation, and death, made merry with the blithest. By the margin of the pond— the length of the Infirmary pond was six hundred and fifteen feet, its width at the Mosley Street end eighty feet, and at Portland Street sixty feet—the fountains in the basin, although unable to rival continental fountains in magnitude or beauty, certainly did their best to sprinkle the passers-by; and when the utmost is done to please us we ought to be grateful. From

·L

three large fountains the water rose glittering to a reasonable height, while the smaller ones displayed a due spirit of emulation."

Another event that the writer will not be likely to forget was the Art Treasures Exhibition of 1857. The paintings by ancient and modern masters, the portrait gallery and museum, the sculpture and sketches which had been got together, exceeded all expectations, and surpassed in value and interest anything of the kind seen before or since.

CHAPTER IX.

ADDRESSES.

OPEN COMPETITION: ITS DEMAND UPON WORKERS.*

I AM glad to meet you again at the annual festival. There have been great changes since our last gathering in January, 1877. Many who then looked upon the opening year with hopeful feelings have had all or almost all their hopes blighted. The condition of the country did not improve as was expected. The year has been a sad one, and the prospect is little or no better to-day. Not only have we had to meet increased competition at home, but also the keener competition of manufacturers in other countries, who have all our appliances, who work longer hours for less money, and, further, utilise the labour of children to a far greater extent than is considered right or prudent in England. Look at the circumstances as we will, condemn some things as we may, the facts are here, and we must continue to suffer for some time a loss in many branches of trade. I earnestly hope and believe that, as the people of other countries become more enlightened in free-trade principles, we shall see the

---

* Delivered at Crewe, January, 1878, on the occasion of the annual entertainment given by Messrs. Rylands and Sons to their employés, at the Longford Works, Crewe.

almost prohibitive tariffs reduced or abolished, and
shall be allowed to deal on a common mutual basis,
each country supplying to the other what it can best
produce.   I feel that the significance which formerly
attached to the word foreign has almost gone ; our
communication by telegraph bringing us practically as
near to France and Germany, Belgium, Norway, Den-
mark, and the States of America as to our clients in
Northumberland and Cumberland.   As regards our
friends on the continents of Europe and America, their
visits are as common and as frequent as those of our
customers in some parts of Ireland and Scotland.
Why, then, should there be any other than a mutual
principle of goodwill, and honest, open competition,
the best and most industrious securing the reward of
their diligence and labour ?   I would ask you seriously
to consider our present position.   Up to a recent date
we were head and shoulders above all others in our
power of production.   Shall we allow ourselves permanently to lose that position ?   If not, our labour must
be brought more and more into harmonious action
with capitalists, and both must prepare for some sacri-
fices.   If this be done, a future even greater is in store
for us.   The trade of China, of India, and of Africa,
would ere long exceed in magnitude and importance
all the past, and if we secure the confidence of these
great nations, by means of honest goods and fair prices,
we shall have a reward for all our anxiety and efforts.
As to our own great business firm, we feel our responsibility, and mean to do our part in the keen struggle.
A few days ago I was reading a book entitled *The Life*

of Sir Titus Salt. One evening he was entertaining a number of distinguished guests, and one of them said: " Sir Titus, what book are you reading or studying just now?" He replied, " Alpaca; and if you had to provide for the daily wants of four thousand to five thousand people, you would find that full occupation." I fancy that if we heard the same learned professor put the same question to the governor and head of our firm, the reply would be, " Cotton" or "New High Street;" and, after a pause, he would add, "and if *you* had to provide for the daily needs and comforts of eleven thousand to twelve thousand people, you would find that small, absorbing volume worthy of your greatest powers and closest attention." Whilst we are reading daily of the valour and bravery of the soldiers on the battle-fields, let us remember that there are heroes and heroism in commerce, and that we have them in our midst. I would ask you to second the efforts of our managers in the ready-made branch of our business, which constitutes a busy line of industry in Crewe; and let us all, whatever our position, try to place the company in a higher state of prosperity and usefulness. The great progress made in railways and telegraphs has brought continental nations into still closer competition with us, and competitors from continental nations are frequently in the Manchester markets against us; and therefore we should never relax our efforts, but join the masters in the endeavour to maintain that supremacy which English goods enjoy for quality and cheapness.

FURTHER FACILITIES FOR COMMERCIAL TRAVELLERS.*

We are told, and I think with some degree of truth, that we shall see an improvement in trade this year. The requirements of our colonies and America, which have been favoured with good harvests, are so largely in excess of the past few years, that, in spite of our expensive government and bad harvests, we shall have more occupation for our people in the coal and iron fields. This will react upon our textile manufacturing districts, and the country will generally feel a change for the better. But we must not be too sanguine. The losses this empire has sustained through the failure of the crops for the last four years are so serious that we cannot recoup them but by slow degrees. It is, however, our duty to do all we can to help on the development of our trade in every way, and especially by preparing to meet the competition of other nations which are trying to take some branches of trade from us. In addition to the benefit arising from cheap food and the lower price of all dress materials and household necessities, much good has been effected of late by the people of this country adopting more economical habits. The saving has been considerable, and has done something towards making up the national loss occasioned through our having to pay Canada and America for corn, which,

---

* Delivered at Crewe, January, 1880, at the annual gathering of Rylands and Sons' employés.

with more favourable weather, we should have reaped from our own land. It is most desirable that the saving habits of the people should be fostered and encouraged ; and I would that our friends should avoid the drinking and smoking which are so common amongst the young people of our large cities and towns, and use their money in purchasing such things as will find more and better employment for workmen. I shall not dwell more largely upon this subject. Had we been favoured with the presence of the governor of the company (Mr. Rylands), he would have done so, and more effectually, from his long and varied experience in commercial matters. Nor shall I speak in this mixed assembly on politics. I have my own convictions as to the conduct of her Majesty's advisers during the past crisis, but this is not the time or place to give expression to them. But, if you will permit me, as I am before a large number of commercial men, and in the town in which are situated the offices and works of the greatest railway company in the world, I will say a few words upon the subject which is occupying the attention of a large portion of the commercial community, and which is of vital importance to our manufacturers and merchants—I mean the facilities, or rather the want of facilities, for transferring from one part of the country to the other, by means of commercial travellers, upon our railways, the various products of foreign and home manufacture. At the time the regulations for traffic were established, and the special provision for passengers' luggage made, they were fairly in accordance with the then requirements both of private

passengers and of commercial travellers; but, as years
rolled on, the commerce of the country largely increased,
and the various companies wisely and kindly resolved
to relax the stringent regulations as they affected the
weight of luggage allowed to the commercial traveller.
But an allowance which a few years ago was thought
liberal has now become absolutely unequal to the requirements of the gentlemen who represent the various
mercantile firms of London, Birmingham, Manchester,
and other centres, whose business now requires, instead
of ten or fifteen representatives, with $1\frac{1}{2}$cwt. to $2\frac{1}{2}$cwt.,
in many instances not less than twenty to forty travel-
lers, each carrying such a variety of patterns that they
cannot be compressed in less than an average of 4cwt.,
which is in excess of the weight permitted by the
railway companies. It must be remembered that these
gentlemen are not only spending large sums of money
in travelling as passengers, but are taking with them
samples and patterns of various manufactures special
to each district, thereby creating a trade in every
county into which they enter, cultivating taste, and
developing every branch of business, from that of the
humblest shop to that of the palatial warehouse and
hotel, thereby enlarging the luggage traffic of the
various railway companies to an extent the magnitude
of which we can scarcely comprehend.   We, therefore,
ask that in future each commercial traveller should be
allowed to carry patterns and samples as follows :—
If travelling first class, 4cwt.; second class, 3cwt.; third
class, 2cwt.; to be excessed above this limit up to 2cwt.
at the rate of a halfpenny per mile; and we respectfully

suggest that the bye-laws giving the officials power to double the excess charge, if the ticket be not taken at the commencement of the journey, should be rescinded. The adoption of these proposals would be a boon to the great body of commercial travellers, would undoubtedly save a great deal of annoyance, attack if not destroy a source of corruption which is demoralising to all parties concerned, and secure without doubt a much further increase in the traffic of the country. It cannot be questioned that the daily exhibition of new goods in new designs, of home and foreign production, by a body of thirty thousand to forty thousand travellers all over Britain, amongst thirty millions to forty millions of people, must create a much larger trade, and, consequently, augment the revenue of each railway company. Of course it will be necessary that each firm should furnish the name, and, if desirable, as in Belgium, the photographs of their representatives to the various companies, and each commercial traveller should be in possession of an ivory or silver ticket; or if, as is suggested, the railway companies should do as the American railway companies, they might give each traveller a yearly book of coupons for a fixed sum, without any restrictions as to weight of samples or patterns; or adopt any other plan which may be found most convenient. A further boon might be granted, and that is giving the commercial travellers return tickets at a single fare on the Saturday, so that, when desired, they might return to their families, and enjoy their well-earned rest and pleasure of the sabbath in their own homes. From my knowledge of our railway

managers and directors, I feel that these matters only
need to be placed before them in a clear and proper
form to secure their adoption; and I join in this
movement the more readily because it will not only
secure a moral and social improvement, but a distinct
and unmistakeable gain to all the railway companies
in point of revenue.

RAILWAYS A CIVILISING FORCE.*

I would remind you that you are living in a town
which is now widely known.   The rapid growth of the
population of Crewe during the last twenty or thirty
years has been remarkable, and it was only in just
recognition of its position amongst the thriving and
populous towns of the country that it was placed on
the list of municipal boroughs.   The way in which the
members of the corporation had discharged the important and responsible duties of their position had
shown the wisdom of this arrangement, and had resulted
in a new and improved state of things in the borough.
We are favoured this evening with the presence of
your chief magistrate, and you will, I am sure, join
with me in giving him a hearty welcome.   The great
railway company which gives employment to so large
a portion of the population of Crewe is deserving of
our highest appreciation; but we must not forget the
other firms and companies who, seeing the character

---

* Delivered at Crewe, December, 1881, at the annual meeting of
Rylands and Sons' employés.

of the Crewe people, and knowing that there was a
large number of unemployed females, had come and
established places of business in their midst, finding
occupation for those who would otherwise have led
comparatively useless lives, and in many cases have
been a burden to their parents and families. It is also
pleasing to hear from those amongst you who are
capable of forming an accurate judgment that, apart
from trade and its immediate surroundings, there are
many signs of progress to be found in your institutions,
both literary, scientific, and political, and, I may add,
religious also. This development will, I hope, be more
manifest as years roll on; and I trust that you will
rise still higher in the social scale, and become a centre
of light and power in the county of Chester. You will
pardon me now if, for a short time, I refer to a matter
which affects the trades, both wholesale and retail, of
all towns, namely, the carriage of parcels by post and
by passenger trains. Your worthy mayor will at once
see the importance of the effort we are making to
secure a postal service to all parts of the empire, taking
parcels up to four pounds weight for a small charge.
Some say we should press for seven pounds, but at
present we are aiming at four pounds only; and if this
is secured it will be found an immense boon to all
parties. Then we shall go to the railway companies
and ask them to grant a concession, and allow parcels
up to twenty-eight pounds to be sent by passenger
trains at a low charge, according to distance. From
careful enquiry, we feel convinced that the result will
be a great advantage to the railways, and a great help

to traders throughout the kingdom. We appeal to the railway companies to meet this just and business-like request. We must remember that railways are in a sense a monopoly. They are not simply to be looked upon as dividend-making institutions. They are great factors in the development of our national life. They are essential to our position if we are to maintain our commercial standing. Nay, more, the supplying of the very needs of the people, socially and mentally, depends largely upon them. The changes which the introduction of the railway system has wrought in this country cannot be stated or estimated. The current of thought is changed, the habits and customs of the people are improved, the style of dress, aye, and even the very language of our rural population have been materially altered. Now-a-days you do not ask men *how* they can move this or that weight of material; but what it will cost, and which is the best company to send it by. You do not ask the distance from town to town; but how long will it take by such a train. We do not discuss about the time *when* we shall be able to see such and such a book or paper; but it is ordered to be here or there in the morning. The railways are in this and also in other ways a great civilising force. They have done in large measure in India what all the talking of sages and good men could not have effected in a century, they have helped to break down caste. Men of different castes, who used to walk apart from each other, as far apart as the width of a street, and would not meet in any room, now rub together as they get their railway tickets, and, to save the difference between first and third class fares, will all ride together third class. They have found out that it makes no difference to them morally or physically; that they are just the same whether they touch each other or not; and so, in a while, it is to be hoped that they will, by receiving further light, discover that they have one common Father and one common home above. Much more might be said if time would permit, but I will not detain you further. The railways should be deemed to be on a higher platform than ordinary business ventures; the public wants should be consulted, every convenience consistent with justice and reason should be afforded, and the request now put forward is certainly within their power to grant; and the granting the same would add one more to the many wise and prudent changes that have been made for the general good.

PERSONAL REFERENCES TO MR. RYLANDS. BUSINESS AND THE WORKERS.*

I am sure you are highly gratified to have had the presence this evening of the governor of the company. I have a vivid recollection of the time when Mr. Rylands' voice would have reached the utmost corner of this great hall, and his speech would have held the audience spell-bound. I am sure you have been pleased to see his healthy appearance, and to hear a gentleman of his age speak so happily and encourag-

---

* Crewe, January, 1884.

ingly.   It was my pleasure to be present a few days ago at the annual meeting of the Benevolent Society, established for the benefit of the packers and porters in the employ of our company in the Manchester warehouse.   On that occasion our worthy chief, Mr. Rylands, presided.   Standing up before that assembly of strong, hearty men, who had rendered faithful service to the firm for many years, he said: " I have been on this spot sixty-two years.   I was the most delicate child my mother had."   At the mention of his mother his heart swelled with emotion, and he who had toiled and succeeded, amid difficulties and trials which would have crushed most men, stood there before that meeting with tears in his eyes, incapable for the moment of expression.   There is a tenderness of influence about a mother that never forsakes a child.   Though there may be a temporary waywardness, a course of evil living, some day, sooner or later, the mother's kindness and her early entreaties will subdue the heart, and call forth feelings of contrition.   Mr. Rylands had a joyous recollection of his beloved parent.   The other day I read a story of a wealthy merchant who had been a worldly man, and had purchased a lot in a new cemetery and wished to remove the remains of his mother, who had been dead twenty years.   He superintended the transfer himself, and the occasion was a most affecting one for him.   The memories of his mother came up afresh, and her pious and faithful life revived before him after a silence and absence of twenty years with new significance and expressiveness.   He thought of her prayers for him, and every remembered incident, which told of her affectionate care and Christian dutifulness, had a voice in it that addressed his conscience as powerfully as it touched his heart. He bowed to the blessed influence, and became a follower of his mother's God. Returning, however, to the meeting. Mr. Rylands said: " I have never passed one year without a profit financially, and I hope, though I don't like to speak of myself, there has been no year without some record for good; and, further, I can say there has not been any year or any time during the whole period since 1827 that I have been away from business for forty-eight hours either through carelessness or illness." That was a great deal to say. And though it is not to be expected that you or I, or one out of ten thousand ten times told, can accumulate the wealth or acquire the wide influence in the commercial world which is now held by the governor of the company, yet we can all of us try to be faithful in the discharge of our duties, embracing every opportunity for good and useful work which our position, our capacity, and our strength may enable us to perform. Those who seek and desire opportunities for good work will find them. Many of you who are here are from happy homes, where parents and brothers and sisters live with joyous surroundings. But, remember, some even in this town, and many in our large cities, are without those joys, comfortless, and utterly neglected; and though it is the duty and the pleasure of large corporate and educational bodies, whether looking at it as a matter of social ethics or of economy, to care for the fatherless and the destitute and neglected, it is

a much higher pleasure, a holier and more blessed
privilege, for a child to receive its direction from a
loving parent, and to find its first impulses and energies guided by a father's and mother's hand and heart,
or, if not by them, by a kind and loving friend.   Now,
as to what you young folks are doing here amongst
yourselves.   You have done a good thing in establishing your sick and benevolent society.   I think you
might also with advantage establish a savings bank, if
not within your own place, then in connection with the
Post-office Savings Bank.   So many of our young
people get married, that it is of the utmost importance
to begin to save at once what little they can afford.   It
will be found a most valuable help for them when they
come to furnish their new home.   It is unnecessary to
provide clubs or reading-rooms.   These, with other
conveniences for lectures and concerts, have been so
amply and fully provided for the population in your
mechanics' institutions, and in connection with your
churches and chapels.   I have been asked whether I
object to young people enjoying a dance or a dramatic
performance.   My reply is, certainly not.   So far as
children are concerned, they cannot help dancing; and
I know no exercise so pleasing or graceful for young
men or women as dancing.   But it should be kept in
moderation.   As to theatres, I know there are many
temptations in and around them which are inimical to
a simple Christian life.   Many of the evils could be
and ought to be remedied, and a higher moral tone
given and maintained.   The theatre might then become
one of the great training schools for the young and

middle-aged of both sexes. John Locke, the writer, says: "All plays and innocent diversions, so far as they contribute to my health and consist with my improvement, condition, and with my other more solid pleasures of knowledge and duty, I will enjoy; but no further." All reasonable and proper sources of enjoyment we recommend, for we want our workpeople to be strong, bright, and cheerful. Hearty, healthy boys and girls or men and women will do better for themselves and for their employers than dull and unhealthy people. Your workrooms are healthy, they are light, airy, and convenient, and we ask you to utilise all other means at your command in such a way as shall contribute to a cheerful and happy life. You are engaged in a business which is as permanent and as enduring in its character as humanity itself. Undoubtedly there are still many people in distant warm countries where clothing is scantily used, where the beautiful figures of woman and her companion are still unadorned, and care not for our productions; but their number is growing less. Civilisation is extending, taste for dress is increasing amongst all people in every clime; and amongst the skilled artisans and the enterprising manufacturers and merchants who supply the markets we intend to hold our place; and we confidently believe our reputation as makers of dress goods and articles for domestic use will win for us a still larger share of the business of the world, with its one thousand two hundred millions of human beings and their ever-increasing wants. Referring for a moment to business prospects, we have still to complain, not so much of

M

the volume of trade as of its being so unremunerative; and this, I am afraid, applies to all branches of business. For this, many reasons might be assigned with which you are more or less familiar. Competition is bringing us all to a lower level; indeed, it is placing many good and deserving people in great straits, and unless some restraint is put upon it, ruin must fall upon some deserving merchants and manufacturers. There can be no doubt that, for some years past, unscrupulous and unwise men have been conducting their business on principles altogether at variance with our old notions. They seem to be totally uninfluenced by the possible consequences of their foolish and reckless operations, and the bankruptcy court or necessity for liquidation has not appeared to deter them. The crowd of liquidating debtors has been increasing, and you all know how the class of traders to whom I have referred damage, and, in a large number of cases, embarrass and bring to ruin honest, industrious men. But, if I am not mistaken, the new law of bankruptcy laid down in the bill recently passed, if properly administered, will, in some measure, and I hope largely, change this state of things. It will put a stop to much reckless trading; and to the extent that the punishment and shame due to wicked and dishonourable traders (I can call them nothing else) is vigorously enforced, their number will be decreased, and honest and true men supported and encouraged. I will not, however, open the year with more words indicating gloom and sadness. We have had two better harvests, and the impression on many minds is that we have really better times before us—that we have finished the seven lean years, and that we are going to have seven fat years. I join in this feeling, and trust that, if we are spared and permitted to see each other again next year, we may have a still more cheerful report to give. The railway company's great works at Crewe are employing eight thousand men, and I sincerely hope their trade will increase. The firm of Rylands and Sons is employing eleven thousand six hundred people in the various works connected with the business, and I am sure you will join in the hope for its increasing prosperity.

NANTWICH AND ITS BATHS.*

My friends,—In the name of Messrs. Rylands' firm, I have again the pleasure of wishing you a happy new year. Another point in our history has been reached, and if we look back upon the year 1884 it must be to find out the weak points and see how and where we can improve them. At the commencement of the year many promises were made and many hopes cherished, and we confess some of them have not been realised; still if we were individually brought to the test, though we should speak of some dark days, we should also remember we have had "joys." If there have been fierce fightings, there has also been a season of peace and rest; and as we turn our faces now to the future, let it be with good heart. Let us play the man, and

---

* Address delivered at Crewe, January, 1885.

go on in hope and confidence. I have twice had the pleasure of visiting your neighbouring town of Nantwich, on the last occasion in company with a gentleman who, like myself, had a desire to know more of the town and district, and also to ascertain, if possible by personal experience, the effects of the brine baths, about which we had heard and read much. Before referring more definitely to the baths, allow me to say a few words about the town. Nantwich has a population of about seven thousand, and is situated on the banks of the Weaver, four miles from Crewe, on the Shrewsbury line of the London and North-Western Railway. It is the centre of an interesting group of fine old family mansions occupied by persons of distinction. These are Crewe Hall, Beeston Castle, Peckforton Castle, and Combermere Abbey. The latter has become famous in recent years by its having been made the residence during the hunting season of the Empress of Austria. Leland says: "In the reign of Henry VIII. there were three hundred salt mines open in Nantwich, but in the early part of the seventeenth century they were greatly reduced in number. Other and superior pits were opened in the vale of the Weaver, and having the advantage of water carriage, caused a continuous decline of the Nantwich pits, and ultimately they were abandoned." In reading the history of Cheshire, I was much surprised to find that in the reign of Henry I., in 1113, the town was laid waste by the Welsh; and again, in 1282, King Edward had necessity laid upon him to protect the corn and provisions of the inhabitants against a further approach of the Welsh army. In 1438 the town was consumed by fire, and again in 1583. On the 10th December it chanced, as it is expressed in the parish register, "that a most terrible and vehement fyre, beginning at the Water Lode about six of the clock at night, in a kitchen by brewing, the wynde being very boysterouse increased the said fyre, which verie vehementlie burned and consumed in the space of 15 hours six hundred bayes of buildings, and could not be stayed neither by laboure nor pollice, which I thought good to commend to posterity as a favourable punishment of the Almightie in destroying the buildings and goods onlie; by God's mercie but onlie two persons perished by fyre." In the year 1585 another entry was made in the parish register, which runs thus: "This year passed youre most noble Queen Elizabeth (whom God long preserve), of her royal and princelie bountie, granted a commission under her own hand to make a general collection throughout all the realm of England for the re-edyfying of this town of Nantwich, which liberalitie was collected in the year aforesaid, and this year followinge, the Queen contributing £2,000 herself, together with the necessary timber from the Delamere forests, and a number of the houses then erected remain to this day." I wonder whether anyone in the year 2184, speaking about Crewe and its past history, will be able to point to houses erected at this date—1885— as still existing. I trow not. In 1587 the town was visited with a kind of "frenzie or mad ague." The old town seems to have had a series of troubles in the shape of plague, fire, and pestilence, but it survived

them all.   At one time it was an important garrison,
and was always loyal and firm in its devotion to
Parliament.   There are a number of interesting old
buildings which I cannot stay now to describe, but
I must make reference to the grand old church.   It
is a structure in the Gothic-Decorated style of architecture, with a fine octagonal tower rising from the
centre.   Passing some good business premises, which
would do credit to many principal streets in our large
towns, we came to High Street, and at the lower and
extreme end adjoining the river we found the Town
Hall—a large and somewhat handsome building, at
the back of which the brine baths are situated.   Going
through the hall, which seems to be used for a
variety of purposes, we entered the bath buildings.
The town, as I have already stated, is pleasantly
situated, surrounded by many places of interest easily
reached on foot by pedestrians or visited in short
drives, and would, therefore, to our minds, warrant an
effort being made to accommodate individuals or
families wishing for temporary residences to secure the
benefit of the baths.   The building known as the town
hall could be adapted to the purpose with a moderate
outlay, and if I may be pardoned for making a sugges-
tion, it would be that the company should enlarge with
the understanding that after all proper expenses are
paid and five per cent per annum given to the shareholders, the residue, if any, should be handed over,
under the direction of the shareholders through the
board of directors, to the various charities of the town
such as now exist or may hereafter be established for

the education and the moral and social improvement of the people. Of course, I am assuming it would be a fully-licensed hotel, but it being no profit to the proprietors to push the sale of wines and spirits, I apprehend they would be little used. As to the effect of the brine baths I cannot speak from personal experience, but if I may express an opinion formed upon what I have read of the Nantwich, Droitwich, and other brine baths, their curative qualities must be very unmistakeable. One of our medical gentlemen says we have only to turn over the leaves in the book of nature, and there we shall find a remedy for every ailment, an antidote for every poison. The time, he says, is fast approaching when the use of drugs will almost die away, and the various medicine given for different diseases will be to a great extent supplanted by the use of brine baths, diet, and hygiene. These baths, they say, will cure almost all diseases to which poor humanity is liable. In his extreme anxiety to enforce this fact, one doctor in a pamphlet which I read cries out in a sort of agony, " Oh, that the muse of some departed orator would inspire my pen so that the emphasis I lay upon the great value of Nantwich brine might be accepted," and then he goes on to say in reference to cholera, the frightful disease which has been so devastating the Continent during the year just closed, " When I have tried almost every medicine and failed, so surely do tepid brine baths act as an almost certain cure." It was the extraordinary cures effected by taking several cholera cases to the saltworks and placing the patients in the hot brine that led to the

establishment of brine baths at Droitwich, which have
been of gradual but sure growth since that period.   A
correspondent of the *Daily Chronicle* writing on this
subject says, " It is much too simple for some of the
medical men to believe in it; when their medicine fails
they send their patients to Hamburg and Wiesbaden.
Why, are not the waters of Abana and Pharpar far
better than Jordan?"   Of course, they must go to
Germany and France.   Nantwich and Droitwich are
only a few hours from London, and less from the great
centres of Lancashire and Yorkshire.   But the friends
at Nantwich and Droitwich must not be disheartened.
They will gain popularity and success by the report of
those who have found relief from their afflictions.
There remains one other and the crowning virtue of
brine baths which you people of Crewe and we of
Manchester will find the most important addition to
our present character, influence, and future usefulness.
One good doctor says they strengthen the backbone.
I don't know whether your friends at Crewe suffer
much from want of backbone, but I tell you unhesitatingly there are many in our city who do, and I urge
them one and all to visit the Brine Baths at Nantwich
at the earliest possible period, for depend upon it if the
present competition continues we shall not only want
a new stimulus to our frames, but we shall also require
more moral backbone, and I may add a wider and
better knowledge of geography to discover new fields
for our enterprise, and more genius to devise new and
beautiful goods which shall win their way into the
various markets of the world against foreign competi-

tion. It has always been and I hope will continue a characteristic of our firm that we keep abreast of the times and meet the requirements of the trade in all matters pertaining to textile manufacture and clothing. We have hitherto held the foremost position as cotton manufacturers. We own what we believe to be the largest bleaching and finishing works in Great Britain, probably in Europe. We could in a few days encircle the globe with our productions. In calico, in clothing, our output is very large; in shirt fronts and shirts almost incalculable. Altogether our employés number upward of eleven thousand. We say to-night to you workpeople of Crewe, as to all our assistants in London and elsewhere, "Work on cheerfully, as you have hitherto done, and help us in the battle of competition, and enable us to maintain the ground we have now and have so long and honourably held in the front rank of the great commercial army." Our two great mottoes and trade marks are "Hard to beat," "Not the last." The latter of these is, as you know, taken from Mr. Rylands' family crest, and surely no words could be more appropriate as a commercial motto; but in other respects it is most inappropriate, for he is the last surviving merchant and manufacturer of the long list who started the race with him. He has not only outrun them in the extent of his business, but also in the length of days, and in this he is a living example to us all to work hard and live prudently. You will join me, I am sure, in wishing he may be spared for some years yet.

THE POSSIBILITIES OF TRADE EXTENSION.*

The year 1885 has gone with its many trials and struggles, both commercial and political, and we have commenced a new year with your good wishes and very earnestly and sincerely we return the compliment to you all round this festive board. If I had toasts to propose, the first would be our good Queen, who still continues to reign over the largest empire in the world, extending to one-seventh part of the entire land surface of the globe, and over more than three hundred millions of people—one-fourth of the population of the world. To this territory we have recently made another addition by taking Burmah, bringing us closer to the great empire of China. We are hoping to secure additional trade from the Burmese. They are said to be an enterprising people, and occupy a rich and fertile district, with three and a half millions of population, and if they commence making railways, as it is hinted they will, we may hope to see a great improvement in the comforts of their people, and an increase of commercial prosperity to the working population of this island. From China, as you have read, there come good tidings of new enterprises, fresh efforts in the way of increased carrying power, and a better mode of transit both for the people and their productions. It is reported that orders are to be given out to the value of £35,000,000 sterling for materials to be used in the making of their new railways. This, of course, will involve in addition

---

* Address delivered at Crewe, January, 1886.

an enormous outlay in the purchase of land and property, the building of bridges, stations, warehouses, and
the many other erections and conveniences needed for
the working of a great railway system such as they
propose to establish; and when you remember this is
the first departure in that great country from its old
ways, it means a great deal more than at first sight
appears. Bearing in mind that the population of
China is three hundred to four hundred millions, you
will be deeply impressed with the possibilities of a
great nation under such new conditions, though you
cannot possibly contemplate the full effect of the
change. Many of my friends on this platform are old
enough to remember the commencement or the early
period in the working of the railways in this country,
and you know something of the revolution that has
been accomplished, changing all our old notions,
quickening and enlarging all our activities and our
thoughts, creating new industries—in fact, remodelling
the business operations of every county in the kingdom.
There are many incongruities and inconsistencies in
the working of British railways which will be remedied
by-and-by; but the outcome of this great system or
enterprise, on which has been expended no less a sum
than £800,000,000 of money, has been an incalculable
national benefit, and what may we expect to be the
result of such a movement in a nation with such an
enormous population as China? Do you not think we
in Lancashire and Cheshire will secure some benefit
from this new life began in a country which, though
occupied by an ancient and proud people, is yet not

sufficiently advanced in commercial pursuits or scientific and engineering skill to meet the requirements of the new trading communities which will necessarily arise under the stimulus thus given? And if the Government of China, in addition, will take off some or all of the restrictions placed upon our commerce throughout their great empire, it will tend not only to the further-ance of our general commercial interests, but to the lifting of the manufactures of Lancashire from a dis-tressed condition into a position of prosperity, and so I desire to begin this new year with the tree of hope still in bloom—a tree which gives cheerfulness to every person and every home where it is cherished, just as a good character and a manly and womanly life cheer and benefit all who come within the range of their benign influence, whether in the home, the workshop, or the town. I will now conclude, expressing to you the good wishes of Mr. Rylands, and I hope, as I am sure you do, that he may be spared to us for some time yet, and that the directors and all interested in our great company, both in Manchester, London, Crewe, and other centres of operation may be enabled to bring this year's trading, notwithstanding the fierce competition, to more satisfactory results than the one that has just closed.

The Rev. A. W. Potts said he thought it was a very good arrangement that, at least once a year, the em-ployés of Messrs. Rylands and Sons at Crewe should come into contact with the directors of the firm and the heads of departments, and look upon the faces of those who direct these operations in Manchester. They had no less than three directors of the firm present, and ten managers of departments. He regarded it as an excellent thing that business men, such as these gentlemen were, should come over from Manchester and mingle with those whom they employed. It had been a pleasure to him to listen to the remarks about the opening up the immense possibilities of future trade with Burmah and China, and he hoped that Messrs. Rylands would get some of that trade when it came into operation, and if it came to the firm at Manchester, no doubt some of it would come to the works at Crewe. While they had these visions of business he was reminded that Messrs. Rylands wanted their good wishes and co-operation, and he was sure they were ready, not only to offer their good wishes, but to give good work when it was put into their hands to accomplish. The chairman had spoken of the tree of hope. It would be a good thing if it would blossom more frequently, not only at Crewe but elsewhere. It was their hope that the present depression would speedily pass away, and that they would have plenty of work, not only at Messrs. Rylands' factory, but full time in the Crewe Railway Works. He was sure those visions of railway plant and men wanted, which the chairman had referred to, were most entrancing to them, and he trusted that when these works came on for fulfilment they would give employment to many fathers and sons. He wished the firm of Rylands and Sons every prosperity, and that that prosperity might be shared in by their branch at Crewe. He hoped the year upon which they had now entered would be a good, happy, and peaceful year, and that they would all find food and clothing and all which they required.

PRIZE DAY AT CHEADLE HULME ORPHAN SCHOOLS.*

The annual presentation of prizes to the children in the Manchester Warehousemen and Clerks' Orphan Schools at Cheadle Hulme took place at the schools on the afternoon of Saturday last. There was a large gathering of friends, who were delighted with the part-songs sung by the scholars. Mr. Joseph Broom, chairman of the executive committee, presided, and there were also seated on the platform the High Sheriff of Cheshire (Mr. James Jardine), Messrs. Reuben Spencer, Thomas Collier, Captain Blathwayt, G. F. East, P. J. Ramsay, William Baldwin, H. N. Ashcroft, and W. H. Dean, secretary.

The Chairman said he had been connected with the schools almost from the date of their establishment many years ago, and he was gratified to be present once more, because to witness the growth of the schools and the magnitude they had attained was one of the greatest pleasures of his life. The generosity of their ex-president, the late Mr. John Rylands, continued during the whole of his life, and he left behind a bequest which would be exceedingly useful to the schools. They had risen to their present position not

---

* Address delivered at Cheadle Hulme, October, 1889, on the occasion of the distribution of prizes at the Warehousemen and Clerks' Schools.

by leaps and bounds, but by quiet perseverance, until, through the munificence of Mr. Rylands, they were not only free from debt, but were really in an excellent position for an educational institution.

Mr. George Board (the principal) read the annual report, which stated that at the Cambridge local examinations, in December last, twenty-four candidates were entered, and of that number the names of twenty-one appeared upon the published lists, seven of them being placed in honours. Percy V. Board, Alfred Molyneux, and W. E. Shelley were distinguished in drawing, the first mentioned having obtained the enviable distinction of being bracketed first in England. The school compared favourably in efficiency with other schools. In the Manchester centre the school passed fifty per cent, at Liverpool sixty-nine per cent, and the whole of the schools of the country sixty-seven per cent, whilst the Cheadle Hulme Orphan Schools passed eighty-eight per cent. The Manchester centre gained honours at the rate of fourteen per cent, Liverpool twenty-two, the whole of the country nineteen, and Cheadle Hulme twenty-nine per cent. When it was remembered that the bulk of the scholars would not naturally be stronger, either physically or morally, than those of other schools from which candidates came, but rather the reverse, these figures were an eloquent testimony to the excellence of the instruction and training which the schools were calculated to give. In the science and art examinations in May, two hundred and forty-one certificates were gained by seventy-five individual scholars. In order to promote thoroughness

in their teaching the science apparatus of the school
had been recently replenished and increased, and every
step had been taken to secure to the students an expe-
rimental as well as a theoretical knowledge of the
subjects they might happen to take up. The idea of
giving the boys an insight into some kind of manual
instruction during their term of residence had at length
been realised, and the workshop which the committee
were able to devise and construct had now been supplied with eight complete sets of tools, through the kindness of a Manchester gentleman, and everything was
in readiness for the sympathetic training of batches of
the most apt and deserving of the pupils in the elementary knowledge of a handicraft. The athletics of
the school had not been lost sight of, the gymnasium
having been extended, and it was now most complete
in every respect. The health of the scholars latterly
had been uniformly good, and all signs of the epidemic
of scarlet fever, which affected the welfare of the institution for so long, had altogether disappeared. The
committee had not been unmindful of future contingencies, and additional hospital accommodation had
been provided, so that they might be able to cope with
any attacks of infection should they happen to occur.
They had accomplished the erection of a new infirmary,
amply sufficient to meet all reasonable requirements.
There would, therefore, be no necessity to send patients
to the Stockport Borough Hospital in future.

After handing the prizes to the scholars, the writer
gave a short address. He said he assumed that the
ladies and gentlemen present that afternoon were very

closely connected with this city. The directors and managers of these noble schools were all Manchester men. They belonged to a city which he held to be second only to the metropolis. He was happy to state that the movement for the education of the people had taken a deep hold on the sympathy of our citizens. As a father of a number of sons, he knew from experience the cost of education in public schools, and, judging from the excellent report, which showed the success of many of the children of this great institution, he took it that they would not be afraid to be tested against most of the schools of front rank. He rejoiced in their prosperous condition and healthy surroundings, but he could not refrain from the expression of regret that there should be one person among the higher class of Manchester warehousemen or clerks who should be so forgetful of his important duty as to neglect this grand opportunity for procuring at a small cost the inestimable boon of education and protection here provided for his children should they require them. He would remind the company and all other people that the future of this country was going to be very different to the past. The young fellows who were now enjoying the wealth of their fathers, and using their time for no practical purpose, would find society in a very altered condition twenty or thirty years hence, and unless they realised their responsibilities they would have to stand aside and let the new life, the well-educated youth of to-day, go to the front. The next generation or two would make the ground very hard for idlers. He esteemed very highly the intelligent men in all pro-

N

fessions, but the young people in these schools would for the most part be thrown into the business world. He did not mean Manchester warehouse life, about which there was a foolish mania, but the various branches of business. What was meant by being devoted to business? Was it, as some said, a hum-drum life? He replied no. Every intelligent faculty a man possessed could find full scope in a business career, every truly philanthropic spirit, every moral instinct, every impulse of a manly soul, could there find ample room for exercise. Young people should have plenty of time for play, and a fair time for the use of the tools in the shop of the joiner or mechanic. He wished to warn them with special reference to two things. In the first, he would impress upon them the paramount importance of truthfulness, and in the second to avoid gambling. His opportunities for observation amongst young people were very considerable, and he assured them that the most horrible thing he knew of in connection with Manchester was the habit of gambling, which was carried on to an extent no one present had any conception of.

CHAPTER X.

JOTTINGS.

SOUTH AND SOUTH-EAST AFRICA AND THE MANCHESTER TRADE.

AFRICA, South, East, and Central, has been receiving a large amount of public attention of late; but as the interests of South and South-East Africa are more directly associated with the home-trade houses of Manchester, reference will here be made to those parts only. It is to the Cape and Natal that the youth of Lancashire and some other parts of our country have been going. For a time the tide of emigration was comparatively small, but since the discovery of diamonds in such large quantities, and the more recent finding of gold, the attraction has proved irresistible, and the number of those who have landed on the southern and south-eastern shores of Africa has greatly increased; and now the progressive Britisher is overpowering in number as well as energy the slow-moving Dutch. In place of the old bullock waggons, moving over the ground at a quiet pace, sometimes waiting days for the fall of a river which had been swollen by heavy rains, they have now a considerable and well-organised railway system; and in districts which, a few years ago, had here and there a farmhouse, there are now large towns and important centres of commerce, and our trading with these colonies is becoming a matter of great importance. The commercial aspect of affairs can be readily seen, and in a succinct and definite form, by the facts as they are reported in the Board of Trade Journal:—

TRADE RETURNS OF CAPE COLONY.

A return of the trade of Cape Colony for the year ended June 30th, 1889, compared with the year ended June 30th, 1888, compiled by the Collector of Customs at Cape Town, has been published by the Assistant Treasurer of the Colony.

According to this return the total value of the imports for the year ended June 30th, 1889, was £9,240,515, representing an increase of £2,867,258 over the amount for the previous twelve months, when it was £6,373,257. The import value of ordinary merchandise was £6,336,801 (an increase of £1,191,052); of colonial government articles, £311,230; of imperial government articles, £9,827; and of specie, £2,582,657 (an increase of £1,509,218).

The exports for the year had a total value of £9,272,992, against £8,223,861 in 1887-88, an increase of £1,049,131. £4,438,205 represents the value of the produce of the colony exported (exclusive of gold, diamonds, and specie); this is an increase of £818,421 over the previous twelve months. The value of gold exported was £697,130, showing the large increase over the £263,626 for 1887-88 of £433,504. Diamonds exported through the Post Office, Kimberley, had an aggregate value of £4,007,866 (a decrease of £219,110); and specie, £129,791.

The amount of custom duties collected was £1,132,661, an increase of £126,327.

Two thousand one hundred and eighty-three vessels, with a tonnage of 3,382,370 tons, entered inward in 1888-89, being an increase of three hundred and fifteen in the number of ships, and of 564,539 tons in the tonnage.

Vessels cleared outward to the number of two thousand one hundred and sixty-seven, with a tonnage of 2,361,537 tons, representing an increase of three hundred and twenty-one in the number of shipping, and of 545,649 tons.

REVENUE RETURNS OF CAPE COLONY.

From a return issued by the Assistant Treasurer of Cape Colony, on July 26th, 1889, it appears that the amount of unaudited revenue received during the year ending June, 1889, was £3,837,220, representing a net increase of £410,858 over the previous twelve months. The principal items of revenue are railway receipts (£1,538,694) and Customs (£1,133,121).

TRADE AND SHIPPING RETURNS OF NATAL, FOR FIRST SIX MONTHS OF 1889.

From the report of the Collector of Customs at Port Natal, relating to the first six months of the present year, it appears that the total number of steamers and sailing vessels entered at Port Natal during that period was two hundred and thirty-six, with a tonnage of 231,188 tons. The figures for the corresponding period of 1888 were two hundred and fourteen ships and 162,595 tons. Imports show a considerable advance, from £1,313,133 in 1888 to £1,813,893 in 1889. The Customs revenue amounted to £161,748 this year, against £128,144 last. In the number of tonnage of steamers and sailing vessels cleared outwards there is also a marked increase over 1888, the figures being two hundred and forty-three ships with a tonnage of 230,462 tons, as compared with two hundred and six ships with a tonnage of 160,977 tons. Compared with 1888, the total exports for the first half year of 1889 also exhibit an increase, the total value of the latter being £975,792, as against £705,419 for the former.

RAILWAYS IN NATAL.

The following information respecting the railways of Natal is extracted from the report of the Governor on the Blue Book of that colony for the year 1888:—

The number of miles of railways open in Natal on

December 31st, 1888, was two hundred and thirty-three and a half. The lines, which are single ones of 3ft. 6in. gauge, are all the property of the colonial Government. Elands Laagte, the furthest point to which the railway is open on the main line, is two hundred and five miles from Durban, and sixteen miles from Ladysmith, the present general terminus for goods. The section to Biggarsberg Summit, about twenty-six miles from Elands Laagte, is expected to be open for traffic in July, 1889, and the next section, about thirty-seven miles, to Newcastle, will probably be completed by the end of 1889. The extension from Newcastle to Coldstream, on the Transvaal border, about thirty miles, will probably be open for traffic by the middle of 1890. The extension of the railway from Ladysmith to the border of the Free State at Van Reenen's Pass in the Drakensberg is about to be commenced, and will be proceeded with as rapidly as possible.

The revenue of the railway department for 1888 showed, after deducting working expenses, a contribution of interest at the rate of £5. 7s. 6d. per cent on the capital expenditure, as against £3. 2s. 2d. per cent in 1887.

PRIMITIVE METHODS OF EXCHANGE, WITH NOTES ON CURRENCY AND BANKING.

Money is a term used to describe any article or commodity, which the people of any nation may agree to receive as an equivalent for their labour or anything else they have to sell or dispose of. A remarkable and interesting variety of materials have been used in different countries at different periods of their history.

It is related in the *Encyclopædia Britannica* that the ancient Russians and Wild Indians of the old unculti-vated part of America used the skins of wild animals as money. In a pastoral state of society, cattle are most commonly used for that purpose. Homer tells us that the armour of Diomede cost only nine oxen, whilst that of Glaucus cost one hundred. The ety-mology of the Latin word *(pecunia)*, signifying money, and of all its derivatives, proves that cattle *(pecus)* had been the primitive money of the Romans. They had also been used as such by the ancient Germans; for their laws uniformly fixed the amount of the penalties to be paid for particular offences in cattle. In remoter ages corn was very generally used, in agricultural countries, as money; and even within the last thirty or forty years it has been by no means uncommon to stipulate for corn rents and wages. Other commodities have been used in different countries. Salt is said to have been the common money of Abyssinia; a species of shells, called cowries, from the Hindu Kauri, the *Cypræa moneta*, gathered on the shores of the Maldive Islands, are used in smaller payments throughout Hindostan, and form the only money of extensive dis-tricts in Africa.

Dried fish was the money of Iceland and Newfound-land; sugar of some of the West India Islands; and Dr. Smith mentions that there was, at the period of the publication of the *Wealth of Nations*, a village of Scotland where it was customary for a workman to carry nails, as money, to the bakers' shops or the ale-house.

Hume, in his essay on money, says: "Whatever may be the material of the money of any country, whether it consist of gold, silver, copper, iron, leather, salt, cowries, or paper, and however destitute it may be of intrinsic value, it is yet possible by sufficiently limiting its quantity to raise its value in exchange."

Money discharges the two main functions of measuring values and mediating exchanges. These uses may be briefly defined. As a measure of values, money removes such of the difficulties of barter as arise from the question of equivalency or price. A trader, under a system of barter, would require to know the prices of everything he needs for use in terms of each of the commodities he possesses to dispose of. If it were possible for a man to have a grocery store where all trading is done by barter, it is easy to realise what his difficulties would be. He will to-day exchange, say, sugar for meat; to-morrow his baker wants sugar and offers him bread; and the day after, his bootmaker; he must know, therefore, the price of sugar in terms of meat, bread, and boots in order to deal with his customers, and so with every article he requires. These same three tradesmen will also want butter, and butter must therefore have its prices in meat, bread, and boots, and so on. The use of money avoids all this complexity; each article has its money value or price, and is paid for in money. This fact is expressed by calling money a measure of values. The second chief use of money is as a medium of exchange. Going back again to barter—the only mode of trading possible apart from the use of some definite substance as money—a man, we will suppose, has a pig to part with, and wants a gun. But he may walk many days before he finds a man who has a gun to part with and wants a pig. Travellers in foreign parts of backward civilisation are often troubled greatly to obtain a meal ; the food-vendor will not dispose of his goods unless the hungry traveller can satisfy him in exchange; hence the number of articles likely to excite the cupidity of the natives which travellers carry with them in order to multiply their chances of suiting the provision vendors and obtaining a dinner. Wherever money is used this diffi-culty is avoided. For the use of money means that one substance is chosen which all are willing to accept in exchange for what they possess, and which therefore gives power, to the full extent of one's possession of it, to purchase any or every article of use. Money becomes the medium or lubricator of exchanges.

The same money need not, however, be both the measure of values and a medium of exchange. It may mediate exchanges without measuring values. Silver in England is used daily in millions of exchanges; it is, therefore, a medium of exchange; but silver is not, in England, a measure of values. Everything has its value measured in gold, even a penny 'bus fare. The man who rides two hundred and forty times has spent,

not two hundred and forty times the value of the
bronze in the penny, but a sovereign. The penny has
a gold value; it represents the two hundred and
fortieth part of the gold unit, which is the standard or
unit of measurement of values. The same is true of all
kinds of convertible paper-money. Bank notes, bills
of exchange, promissory notes, cheques, all represent
gold values. Not they, but gold measures values; they
mediate—and to how great an extent the developments of the banking system testify—exchanges. As
much as ninety-nine per cent of the wholesale trade of
an advanced commercial country like England is
carried on by means of these passports of credit. The
subjoined figures, taken from the Bankers' Almanac for
1889, may therefore be of interest, for banking represents what may be styled the third stage in the history
of exchanges. We have, first, the method of exchange
by barter; secondly, as we have seen, far back in his-
torical times, the introduction and use of money in the
shape of some article in common demand and held in
general esteem; thirdly, the development of credit, a
function now largely centralised in the great banking
establishments, which has grown out of the earlier use
of banks as centres of deposit, trafficing and nego-
tiating in money, receiving it on deposit, and lending
it out at interest.

INCREASE IN BANKING CAPITAL, 1887–88.

The additions to the capital and reserve funds of the banks of the
country during the year 1888 have followed in the main the usual lines.
We give below the usual summary of the position of matters from 1876
to 1887, with an estimate of the main alterations up to October, 1888,

which show a net increase of about £350,000 during the year in the United Kingdom. This is a larger increase than that which took place last year. The amount recorded then was little more than £80,000, while the statement this year compares fairly with the movement in 1886, which showed an increase of about £540,000. The total banking capital of the country may now be placed at about £101,000,000, of which about £70,000,000 is stated as capital, and about £31,000,000 as reserve. The increase this year has practically been almost entirely in the reserve funds in England and Wales.

It will be observed that the reserve funds of the English joint stock banks are now distinctly more than half their capitals, and the position of the Scotch banks is, speaking broadly, similar in this respect.

BANKING CAPITAL IN GREAT BRITAIN AND IRELAND, OCTOBER, 1888.

	Capital.	Reserve funds.
Bank of England £14,553,000		Say, £3,000,000
Other Joint Stock Banks, England. 38,911,600		,, 20,764,500
Joint Stock Banks, Isle of Man ... 91,900		,, 60,500
Ditto Scotland ... 9,052,000		,, 4,631,200
Ditto Ireland 7,163,800		,, 2,635,800
	£69,772,300	£31,092,000
	£100,864,300	

SUMMARY.

Increase in Banking Capital, England and Wales ... £451,658
Ditto   Isle of Man   1,650
Ditto   Ireland   54,518
	£507,826
Less Decrease in Banking Capital, Scotland 161,402
Net Increase in Banking Capital, United Kingdom, between November, 1887, and October, 1888 ... } £346,424

The statement which follows gives a summary of the additions to capital, as well as of the diminutions which have taken place through failures or otherwise up to 1887, the latest to which we can give the completed figures.

PROGRESS OF BANKING CAPITAL AMONG THE JOINT-STOCK BANKS OF THE UNITED KINGDOM, 1876–1887.

Year.	England and Wales. + Increase in Banking Capital.	Isle of Man. + Increase in Banking Capital.	Scotland. + Increase or − Decrease in Banking Capital.	Ireland. + Increase or − Decrease in Banking Capital.	+ Increase or − Decrease in Banking Capital in the Country generally.
	£	£	£	£	£
1876	+ 1,817,610	+ 6,450	+ 208,816	− 124,585	+ 1,908,291
1877	+ 1,383,152	+ 990	+ 462,891	+ 164,093	+ 2,011,126
1878	+ 195,527	+ 2,900	− 1,125,835	− 19,375	− 946,783
1879	+ 1,198,226	+ 20,699	+ 55,992	+ 26,255	+ 1,301,172
1880	+ 2,998,001	+ 1,865	− 3,424	+ 104,763	+ 3,091,205
1881	+ 471,840	+ 2,000	+ 96,591	+ 188,416	+ 758,847
1882	+ 1,000,217	+ 7,000	+ 402,286	− 314,157	+ 1,095,346
1883	+ 2,400,902	+ 27,000	+ 170,705	+ 134,340	+ 2,732,947
1884	+ 2,135,456	+ 2,100	+ 94,466	+ 68,495	+ 2,300,517
1885	+ 1,821,613	+ 800	+ 4,307	− 581,321	+ 1,245,399
1886	+ 311,616	+ 1,450	+ 13,640	+ 217,230	+ 543,936
1887	+ 127,606	+ 1,500	− 107,066	+ 59,634	+ 81,674
	+ 15,861,766	+ 74,754	+ 273,369	− 76,212	+ 16,123,677

An addition of about sixteen millions, if we allow for the destruction of capital caused by the failure of the West of England Bank, has thus been made during the last twelve years to the banking capital of the country. It is to be observed that half of it has been accumulated, either from the undivided profits of the business, or from the premiums paid on new shares.

AVERAGE MINIMUM RATE OF DISCOUNT CHARGED BY THE BANKS OF ENGLAND, FRANCE, AND PRUSSIA FOR THE YEARS 1844-1887.

	Bank of England			Bank of France			Bank of Prussia				Bank of England			Bank of France			Bank of Prussia		
	Per cent.			Per cent.			Per cent.				Per cent.			Per cent.			Per cent.		
	£	s	d	£	s	d	£	s	d		£	s	d	£	s	d	£	s	d
1844	2	10	0	4	0	0	4	6	0	1867	2	10	9	2	14	0	4	0	0
1845	2	13	8	4	0	0	4	7	0	1868	2	1	11	2	10	0	4	0	0
1846	3	6	6	4	0	0	4	14	0	1869	3	4	2	2	10	0	4	2	0
1847	5	3	6	4	19	0	4	17	0	1870	3	2	0	4	0	0	4	17	0
1848	3	14	5	4	0	0	4	13	0	1871	2	17	8	5	14	0	4	3	0
1849	2	18	7	4	0	0	4	1	0	1872	4	2	0	5	3	0	4	6	0
1850	2	10	1	4	0	0	4	0	0	1873	4	15	10	5	3	0	5	1	0
1851	3	0	0	4	0	0	4	0	0	1874	3	13	10	4	6	0	4	7	0
1852	2	3	0	3	3	0	4	0	0	1875	3	4	8	4	0	0	4	14	0
1853	3	13	10	3	5	0	4	5	0	1876	2	12	1	3	8	0	4	3	0*
1854	5	2	3	4	6	0	4	7	0	1877	2	18	0	2	5	3	4	8	0
1855	4	17	10	4	9	0	4	2	0	1878	3	15	8	2	4	2	4	6	9
1856	6	1	2	5	10	0	4	19	0	1879	2	10	4	2	11	10	3	14	3
1857	6	13	3	6	3	0	5	15	0	1880	2	15	4	2	16	10	4	14	10
1858	3	4	7	3	14	0	4	10	0	1881	3	10	0	3	17	6	4	8	6
1859	2	14	7	3	9	0	4	4	0	1882	4	2	8	3	15	4	4	10	3
1860	4	3	7	3	13	0	4	0	0	1883	3	11	4	3	1	5	4	1	0
1861	5	5	4	5	10	0	4	0	0	1884	2	19	1	3	0	0	4	0	0
1862	2	10	7	3	16	0	4	0	0	1885	2	17	7	3	0	0	4	2	5
1863	4	8	2	4	13	0	4	2	0	1886	3	1	0	3	0	0	3	5	8
1864	7	8	0	6	10	0	5	6	0	1887	3	7	0	3	0	0	3	8	4
1865	4	15	4	3	14	4	4	19	0										
1866	6	19	0	3	14	0	6	4	0										
										Average from 1844-87 ...	3	14	4	3	17	6	4	7	2

* Now the Imperial Bank of Germany.

		Average from 1844–62.	Average from 1863–87.
Bank of England	... ...	...£3 16 2	...£3 12 11
Bank of France	... ...	4 4 1	... 3 12 6
Bank of Prussia	... ...	4 7 4	... 4 7 0

It appears hence that the English money market has, on the average of forty-four years, been cheaper than either the markets of Paris or Berlin. During the last twenty-five years, however, the value of money in this country has been more on a level with that in France.

The following extract will be interesting to Manchester readers:—

In *Harrop's Manchester Mercury* for Tuesday, November 12th, 1771, appears the following advertisement: "Notice is hereby given that the Manchester Bank, together with an Office of Insurance from Fire, will be opened on Monday, the 2nd of December, next, under the Firm and Direction of Byrom, Sedgwick, Allen, and Place. N.B.—Agents for the Fire Office in this and the neighbouring counties will be speedily appointed; and Persons insured in other Offices may remove into this free of all expenses." The Bank was located on the site of the premises at the corner of St. Ann's Square, now occupied by the Scottish Union and National Insurance Company. It was opened on the day announced, and on December 3rd Harrop writes as follows: "Yesterday the Bank was opened in this Town under the Sanction of four respectable Gentleman; and from the general Approbation the Scheme has met with amongst all Ranks of People, it is not questioned that it will be of infinite Utility to the Trading Part of the Town, and to the County in general."

The word Bank is said to be derived from the Italian word *Banca*, a bench, benches being commonly used for receiving money in the market places.

STATISTICS OF BANKRUPTCY, 1883–1889.

This is the annual report of the Inspector-General in Bankruptcy:—

The liabilities in cases in which receiving orders were issued in the year ending December 31st, 1888, amount to £7,110,948, and the assets to £2,242,747; showing a diminution in liabilities, as compared with the preceding year, of £1,824,877, and in assets of £424,415. The figures are for England only, not for the United Kingdom.

The following table shows the number of bankruptcies, liquidations or schemes, and compositions, with the amount of liabilities and assets in each year from 1883 to 1888 inclusive.

Year.	Total Number of Cases.	Total of Liabilities.	Total of Assets.	Percentage of Total Assets to Total Liabilities.
		£	£	
1883	8,555	21,268,151	5,987,544	28·1
1884 ⎧ Under Act of 1869	910	3,940,596	898,958	22·8
⎨ ,, ,, 1883	3,260	10,049,399	3,117,040	30·9
⎩ Total	4,170	13,989,995	4,015,998	28·7
1885	4,333	9,037,789	3,093,151	34·2
1886	4,816	7,913,871	2,855,160	36·1
1887	4,839	8,935,825	1,667,162	29·8
1888	4,826	7,110,948	2,242,747	31·5

BANKRUPTCY.

NUMBER OF RECEIVING ORDERS GAZETTED.

	August.		Eight Months ended August.	
	1889. No.	1888. No.	1889. No.	1888. No.
Total gazetted	361	376	3,184	3,310
Number gazetted in the following principal trades and occupations:—				
Grocers, &c.	34	16	247	247
Publicans, Hotel Keepers, &c. ...	19	26	180	226
Farmers	27	20	170	182
Builders	13	28	159	175
Butchers	9	12	111	81
Boot and Shoe Manufacturers and Dealers	9	13	98	112
Bakers	10	9	94	77
Clothiers and outfitters	2	6	28	23
Drapers, Haberdashers, &c.	8	10	83	78
Tailors, &c.	9	3	65	57

INDIAN RAILWAY STATISTICS.

The length of railways open for traffic in India at the end of 1887-88 was 14,383 miles; the length added during 1888-89 was 886 miles. Deducting certain branch lines which have been closed, the total length of open line at the end of 1888-89 was 15,245 miles.

Of the total open line of 15,245 miles, 9,796 miles are worked by guaranteed, assisted, and other companies; 4,998 miles are worked by direct Government agency, and 451 miles are worked by native States.

The total sanctioned mileage on March 31st, 1889, was 17,507 miles, showing an increase over the corresponding figures at the end of the previous year of 637 miles.

THE COTTON MANUFACTURE IN INDIA.

The cotton mills of India employ over 80,000 hands, and with their 18,400 looms and 2,375,379 spindles consumed 2,526,000 cwt. of raw cotton in 1887-88, as against 2,371,000 cwt. in 1886-87.

Spindles in Great Britain	... ...	4,274,600
Ditto Continent ...	... ...	2,333,800
Ditto United States	... ...	1,353,000

	Bales, 400lbs. each.	
	Per annum.	Per week.
Great Britain consumed	... 3,840,000	... 73,860
Continent ditto	... 3,770,000	... 74,500
United States ditto	... 2,590,000	... 49,800

Showing that Great Britain spins the finest yarns.

O

THE PRESS: PAST AND PRESENT.

One of the most remarkable features characterising our modern life, when contrasted with the past, is our daily newspaper. Those among us who remember how in the days gone by we patiently waited for the weekly papers, which were published at fivepence each, containing far less valuable information regarding the state of the markets and intelligence concerning national and local events and foreign affairs than those of to-day, can scarcely realise how quietly and unconsciously we have passed through the transition from the meagre weekly paper to the voluminous morning daily, ever increasing in size and extending the range of news.

ANOTHER CONTRAST OF PAST AND PRESENT CONDITIONS.

We have lived long enough to witness the change from the stage coach, on one of which we first made our entrance into this city, to the railway coach, and we should like to ask our friends, who often complain of some of our third-class carriages, to look at one of the present cattle trucks, open at the top and sides; those are the exact counterpart of the third-class carriages of forty years ago. One was compelled to hold up an umbrella to protect oneself against rain and from the cold winds that pierced through any clothing, and also for the further protection from the smoke, sparks, and soot flying over from the locomotive. The rapid change which has been made, both in the speed and pleasure of riding, can only be understood by those who experienced the old style.

Speaking of the old mode of travelling by coach, we remember an interview we had with two customers, full forty years ago. They were in the office paying their accounts largely in gold. We remarked that it was heavy to carry. "Yes," one of them replied; "you would have thought so if you had had to walk with it in your pocket from Chesterfield to Sheffield to catch the coach. I carried this also," pulling out of his pocket a loaded pistol. "I never come to Manchester without this." The other gentleman exhibited a stick with a dagger inside it, saying, "This is my protector."

To-day, our clients come from this as from all other towns, large or small, by rail, and the moment their account is made out they take from their pocket a cheque-book, and write out a cheque for the amount, and no money of any kind changes hands. In five out of ten cases the cheques are sent by post, saving the customer's time by leaving him every available moment to use in selecting his goods.

STATISTICS OF COACHING BETWEEN LIVERPOOL, MANCHESTER, AND LONDON.

Between the year 1770 and the year 1807 the number of coaches starting out of Liverpool for Manchester and London had increased from two to twenty-seven daily, and the number from Manchester had increased at about the same rate. This increase continued during the whole of the first thirty years of the present century; and between 1825 and 1830 the coaches became so numerous that scarcely a quarter of an hour passed in the course of the day when the rattling of their wheels was not heard along the old Manchester road, and the main reads leading from Manchester and Liverpool towards London.

NOTES ON THE DEVELOPMENTS OF THE MEANS OF COMMUNICATION.

Great as has been the change wrought in the mode of conveyance by the railway, and marvellous as is the change we observe in consequence of the interchange of thought and the new activities arising from the development of the railway system, yet this will be exceeded in all probability by the far-reaching influence of telegraphy, and the use yet to be made of electricity.

The effects already are stupendous. Nothing short of a mighty revolution in the world's commerce has been brought about, and we are but in the infancy of our knowledge as to this factor in the world's work. It affects us in all our relations; it will influence every person and every trade in our country, and will reach every corner of the earth. No man can estimate or prophesy the future of this great motive force; it will be an element to be reckoned with in every new enterprise.

In the early history of telegraphy a company was established to promote the system, proposing to send messages at the uniform rate of one shilling for twenty words, and the writer was amongst the earliest subscribers to the company, feeling confident that it was not only practicable, but would prove most helpful in promoting commerce. The company was not successful for a time; in fact, it reached the very verge of bankruptcy, but the directors were full of confidence as to the prosperity of the undertaking and its ultimate success, and they determined to make a desperate effort to save it from ruin. Two of the board called upon the various shareholders, stating their exact financial position, and the threatened trouble and loss, unless the proprietors could raise so many thousands of pounds within a few days. They allotted to each the due *pro rata* share of the capital to be found. The effort was successful and the position of the company re-established. Shortly afterwards the company's interest was sold to the Government, and the shareholders received a good return for their investments and their courageous assistance in the time of its severe struggle.

When the history of this century comes to be written, electricity will probably be looked upon as the mightiest and grandest of the forces which were brought to bear on our commerce and our general national development.

Lord Salisbury says, in a speech delivered at the annual dinner of the Institute of Electrical Engineers in November, 1889:—

REMARKABLE SPEECH.

I will venture to say that there is no department in the Government so profoundly indebted to the discoveries of those who have made the science of electricity as the Foreign Office. I may say that positively the whole work of all the chanceries in Europe is now practically conducted by the light of that great science, which is not so old as the century in which we live; and it is a strange feeling that you have communicated—constantly and frequently, day by day—with men whose innermost thoughts you may know by telegraph, but whose faces you have never seen.   I have often thought that if history were more philosophically written, instead of being divided according to the domination of particular dynasties or the supremacy of particular races, it would be cut off into the compartments indicated by the influence of particular discoveries upon the destinies of mankind.   Speaking only of those of modern times, you would have an epoch marked by the discoveries of gunpowder, of the printing-press, and of the steam-engine; and those discoveries have had an influence infinitely more powerful, not only upon the large collective destinies, but upon the daily life and experience of a multitude of human beings, than even the careers of conquerors or the devices of the greatest statesmen.   In the list the last competitor is the science of electricity.

I think the historian of the future will recognise that there has been a larger influence on the destinies of mankind exercised by this fascinating discovery than even by the discovery of the steam-engine itself, because it is a discovery that operates so immediately upon the moral and intellectual nature and action of mankind.   The electric telegraph has achieved this great result, that it has assembled all mankind upon one great plane, where they can see everything that is done and said, and judge of every policy that is pursued at the moment the event takes place. By the action of the electric telegraph, you have combined together, almost at one moment, the opinions of the whole of the intelligent world with respect to everything that is passing at the time on the face of the globe.   It is a phenomenon to which nothing in the history of our planet produces anything that is equal, and the intensity of its power increases year by year.   When you enquire what is the effect of the electric telegraph on the condition of mankind, I would ask you to think of the most conspicuous feature in the politics of our time, that occupies the thoughts of every statesman, and places the whole future of the civilised world in a condition of doubt.   It is the existence of gigantic armies, held in leash by the various governments of the world, whose tremendous power may be a guarantee for the happiness of mankind or the permanence of civilisation; but who, on the other side, hold in their hands powers of destruction which are almost equal to the task of levelling civilisation to the ground.   By what power is it that one single will can control these vast millions of men?   It is nothing less than the electric telegraph, and it is on that small discovery that the huge belligerent power of modern states, which marks off our epoch of history from all that gone before, absolutely depends. I do not despair that the distribution of this force may scatter this aggregation of humanity, which it is not one of the highest merits of the discovery of the steam-engine to have produced.

If ever it should happen that in the house of the artisan you can turn on the power as now you can turn on gas—and there is nothing in the essence of the problem, as we know it, to prevent such a consummation from taking place—you will then see men and women able to pursue in their own homes many industries which now require the aggregation of the factory; and you may, above all, see women and children pursue those industries without that disruption of the families which is one of the unhappy results of the present requirements of industry. If ever that result shall come from the discoveries of Oersted and Faraday, you may say that they will have done more than merely add to the physical force of mankind—they will have done much to sustain that unity, that integrity of the family, upon which rests the moral hopes of our race and the strength of the community to which we belong. The point of view from which men of my trade most admire the splendid additions to our energy which the scientific men of the world, and especially of England, in this century have made is that they have enabled mankind to be more happy, more contented, and therefore more moral.

EARLY RECOLLECTIONS OF OLD DEANSGATE AND DIVERS PLACES.

In the early Manchester life of the writer there were two somewhat notorious gardens, one called Whitehouse Gardens, Stretford Road, the other Tinker's Gardens, near Harpurhey.

The journey to Brooks's Bar in those days was an expensive matter; it was looked upon as an important engagement for a Saturday afternoon to ride to the Bar, walking from that point across the fields to the gardens, by the side of the Cornbrook, which at that time was an open stream, crossing what is now Chorlton Road.

Trams, of course, were unknown, and the small, old omnibuses with doors were anything but enjoyable when fairly filled. The omnibuses along old Deansgate took up almost the whole of the space allotted to vehicular traffic. Those who remember Deansgate prior to the alteration well know what a crowded thoroughfare it was, being the busiest part of all Manchester; it was a sight to take friends to see on Saturday nights. The foundation of many a fortune was laid there, and not a few now living are enjoying the fruits of their parents' labours in that remarkably interesting ancient thoroughfare.

Some say the name Deansgate was given to the road which was the line of the march of conquest of the Danes; others say it received the name from the rural dean in the year 634 A.D.; another that its true etymology was Dene, meaning a valley; but, as Mr. Proctor says, it had better be left to the reader to make his choice, and take that which pleases him best.

THE GROWING GAMBLING AND BETTING MANIA.

The trial, on Tuesday, at the Liverpool City Police Court, of the prisoners charged with being concerned in a great racing lottery, called Connolly's, brought forward once more the appalling extent, in this country, of the mania for gambling. This particular lottery business had been pursued for a considerable number of years in connection with horse-racing. Those who had owned and managed it had done so for the benefit of their own interests, not hesitating sometimes to alter the numbers drawn, obviously to defraud those who were entitled to benefit by them. To prevent such rascality becoming known they had occasionally to bribe the men in their employment. The tickets were sold throughout the country by agents, who received as remuneration for their labour a halfpenny for every shilling. The smallness of the rate of the commission seems to have been abundantly compensated for to the agents by the ease and magnitude of their work, owing to the eagerness with which tickets were bought. "Cambridgeshire" tickets were issued to no fewer than thirty-one thousand five hundred people. The detective who had examined the business premises of the concern, stated in evidence at the trial that, since the first day of January last, the total number of tickets issued numbered one million one hundred and sixty-seven thousand two hundred and fifty. These tickets were sold at one shilling each, so that the amount realised from them was £58,362. This by one concern. It is probable there exist many similar firms. Prizes were given to the winning numbers. But they amounted to a trifle of the total sum received. The rest of the money, after paying commission, printing, and other expenses, went into the pockets of the proprietors as profit, which must have been a very large sum. The lucrative character of this business was therefore such as to encourage those who conducted it to go on in spite of the risk of detection and punishment. The sad part of the affair is that so many thousands of infatuated persons were always ready to risk their money, merely for the remote chance of gaining a small prize and for the excitement connected with the expectation of some day realising a hundred, or fifty, or twenty-five pounds, or even less.

Police raids on and prosecutions of high and low betting clubs and associations have served lately to make clear how every class of the community is tainted in one form or another with the ruinous and degrading vice of gambling. In this aspect society is not improving. Moralists have pointed out its evil consequence, mathematicians have calculated the hopelessness to the many of success, preachers have implored old and young to avoid it, and magistrates and judges have denounced it, but all with little effect. Gambling is more rife than ever. It runs through every phase and situation of life. Wherever men and women meet is a stage on which it is practised. There is betting and gambling in kitchens and stables, as well as in drawing, dining, and smoke rooms; in luxurious clubs as in public-houses, in railway trains and in tramcars. Everything is liable to be made the object of a bet or gamble. People bet or gamble on horse-racing, shooting, rowing, stocks and securities of all kinds, billiards, cricket, football, and tennis playing, all sorts of possible events, even those involving life and death, and on domestic, public, or private affairs. No calling or profession is free from it. Statesmen, clergymen, lawyers, magistrates, judges, men and women of property and no property, men whose livelihood is safe and men who don't know how to get their next meal after they have staked their money—all these are its votaries.

This evil is growing. Some forms of gambling and betting have perhaps fallen away, but the worst feature is that there are a greater number of ways now to gratify gambling proclivities than there were, and that these proclivities have developed astoundingly amongst the middle and lower classes. The wretched misery which follows the development of the gambling mania is probably not exceeded by the consequences of any other vice. It unsettles the balance of the mind, provokes irritableness, engenders domestic disquiet. The money which ought to support home in comfort disappears. A race, a fall in stock or shares, a billiard tournament, or a game of cards often leaves penniless even the rich and well-to-do. The agent who sells tickets for a gambling speculation carries off weekly, from the very door of the poor labourer's house, the money which ought to go to feed his children. Escape from the vice is almost impossible when once it has been contracted. Temptation is everywhere. The seller of gambling tickets infests the alehouse and workshop, and even where no professional agency induces gambling, trifling events lead to it, as for instance when a slight difference of opinion arises about any subject, one side concludes the discussion with a challenge to the other to back its opinion with a bet. How gambling leads to drinking and crime has been told too often to need repeating here.

Legislation has tried hard to put effective laws on the statute book. Some of these seem to have changed one form of betting or gambling to another, whilst others have created stirs only spasmodically. Legislation, for instance, gave for a time a blow to betting by rendering bets irrecoverable in courts of law, and by declaring lotteries and sweepstakes illegal. But the professional betting man has overcome his difficulties and raised bookmaking into a fine art, which has evaded the law and especially encouraged horse-racing, until it prevails to an extent to-day that would have staggered the rich men of two generations back with all their individual high play. Of course it would be possible for legislation to meet the professional bookmaker's present position, and so prevent him in his present guise of an agent evading the law; but the bookmaker would soon find ways and means to avoid any new statute.

No law could of course be effective which went so far as to declare gambling and betting in themselves illegal. What can be done as easily in secret as in public cannot be uprooted by mere legislation. A law which proclaimed all gambling illegal would fill the courts with prosecutions and break down. What a host of reputable respectable men would have to be proceeded against under such a law! The speculators in futures, which inflicted on the cotton trade of Lancashire a loss of tens of thousands of pounds this autumn, might under such a law have found themselves in the Liverpool Police Court before they had perfected their "corner." The Stock Exchange would have next to nothing to do, and the incentive to horse-racing would fall to a minimum, if betting and gambling were themselves illegal and severely punishable. Shall betting on horse-racing be prohibited and gambling on cotton futures allowed? Would not an anomaly like this be intolerable? If betting on horse-racing was extinguished, men would find something else to bet upon, just as did the idle miners who in their leisure bet upon which of two worms they had dug out of the ground arrived first outside a circle drawn around them.

It is difficult to see what fresh legislation could do. The law as it exists gives power to remove many public temptations and facilities to betting and gambling. Gaming houses can be put down, and their existence anywhere depends upon the knowledge and vigilance of the police. Many social clubs are no doubt as bad as some houses and clubs used solely for gaming, but they will continue beyond the reach of the law, unless legislation interferes with private life in a way that is sure to irritate people and then bring about a reaction against itself. It has been suggested that publicans should be prohibited from encouraging in their houses betting, as they now do, by exposing sporting papers, obtaining telegrams of the result of contests, races, and games, and by other notable means. The difficulty would, with such a law, be to bring the publican to account. If it is made illegal for them to do any of these things, what is to hinder their customers from exposing a sporting paper or bringing into the public-houses news obtained by telegram of the result of any event? The fact is that, in dealing with betting and gambling by law, beyond prohibiting open and public temptations and facilities to gamble, we are attempting to deal with a phase of life which statute law cannot lay hold of without curbing individual freedom in a way which would disgust people with legislation.

But society has plenty of means at its command to do something towards abating gambling, if it wishes to do so. Newspapers might set themselves against inserting advertisements and articles from tipsters and prophets. Sporting papers could not be expected to do so, but if such advertisements and predictions were kept out of the columns of the ordinary newspaper the influence would be salutary. The upper classes might do much by their example. At present, from the Prince of Wales downwards, a bad example is set the people in gambling and betting. Is it wrong for a prisoner to imagine there is a touch of irony in the denouncement of gambling, which has led to crime, from the lips of a magistrate or judge who himself notoriously gambles and bets? It is of little use calling for legislation against gambling when the heart of the rich and poor is set on it. It is a moral force which wants putting in motion. The old temperance men recognised that lecturing about moderation and abstinence was barren work unless the individual pledged himself to moderation or abstinence. Can nothing in the same direction be done about gambling and betting? Cannot the individual conscience be aroused and pledged against this monster vice? Legislation will never check the mania for hazardous speculation which gives food to a craving for change and excitement, which is felt in this anxious and restless age. The bookmaker and the racing-lottery man does not prepare the ground on which he thrives. The hankering after something, the belief in luck and chance, the hope of a windfall never probable in the ordinary daily round of life, the relief that excitement gives to a monotonous existence all prepare victims for the sharper. Gambling is a terrible social fact, and one that no growling will wipe out, but surely it is not one which society is unable to deal with, if it is willing. But is it willing?—*Manchester City News*, November 2nd, 1889.

THE IMPORTANCE OF LISTENING WITH ATTENTION AND MAKING USE OF JUDICIOUS DISCRETION IN SPEECH.

Amongst the many judicious remarks Mr. Rylands made to us from time to time, one stands out prominently in our memory, and has been useful to us, and we sincerely hope the repetition of it will be of service to others, " Always be a good listener."

Many times we have found the advantage of this. A common habit, especially amongst the younger members of society, but by no means confined to them, is to break in with some observation before the speaker has finished a sentence. We have often experienced the annoyance, and in many cases we are convinced the error arises from the feeling that the person to whom they are speaking has seen a weak point in their remarks, and for fear he should speak about it, they abruptly and foolishly rush in with some observation quite uncalled for; in many cases the expected discovery would never be made if they could but restrain their impetuosity. Besides, when a young man is addressing an elderly person of experience and capacity he must expect to have his weak points found out, for however many weaknesses one may try to repair, others will remain and be seen, and oftentimes more severe remarks are made than otherwise would be if the younger had learned the lesson, "always to be a good listener."

We were once taught a lesson very much on the same lines, and quite as difficult to learn, one that weighed somewhat heavily in its restriction on an active temperament, and was taught at a large creditors' meeting, where there was an unusual number present.

At the meeting there were several barristers, two or three clergymen, several females, a number of merchants, and we think five solicitors. In such a gathering it will be at once assumed there would be much talk, some relevant and some very irrelevant, and as we had previously learned that listening will sometimes evoke the most wonderful information from some men, often from those who are naturally most reserved, we exercised that power to an extent that we thought was commendable.

But as we began to consider the value of the time of business men, and as the particulars brought out seemed to require some explanation, and in one case a rebuke, we were about to speak, but in a moment a hand was placed upon our knee, and turning to the friend, who was one of the oldest and shrewdest solicitors of the city and engaged in the case, he asked us, "Are you going to reply to that man?" We said, "Yes." "Let me advise you," he said, "never speak when the bulk of the meeting is on your side, and it is so now, wait only a few minutes longer." We took his advice, and found it good then, as we have found it many times since.

Difficult as it is to restrain yourself, do so, the result will pay you. All cannot talk well, but all can listen well, if they will make up their minds to do so. In business it is of value, and in society it often lends the opportunity of great and real pleasure.

King Leonidas said to one who discoursed at an improper time, "My friend, you should not talk so much to the purpose of what is not now to the purpose to talk of." Another said, "He who knows how to speak knows also when to speak."

Young salemen are sometimes apt to be impulsive and loquacious. We remember, on one occasion, taking a customer into a department, and asking a young man to serve him. We remained a short time, intending to take the gentleman into another room when he had finished there; he was a large buyer, and deserved special attention. The young man took from the rack certain goods, placed them on the counter, and began a long explanation about the quality of the goods, the warp and weft, the character of the dye, and the reputation of the dyer, their fitness for this and that purpose,—all without being asked a single question. As soon as there appeared to be an opening for an observation, the gentleman, who was a draper of large experience, having been in the trade nearly thirty years, turned to the young man and said: "I am very much obliged for your remarks, but I happened to know a good deal of what you have stated before you were born;" then, without waiting for further remark, kindly said, "Show me the next price." The young man felt his position, and, we think, it was a lesson he would not forget. There are young men just as lethargic and wanting in energy as the one whom we have just mentioned was overflowing and indiscreet. we have many times had to call attention to this fault. If a customer asks for a certain cloth about 4¾d., they will place on the counter one piece at 4⅞d., and say: "That is the nearest we can do, sir," instead of placing quietly, without bustle or noise, three or four pieces at prices varying from 4½d. to 5½d.; a little courteous attention of this kind often effects a sale of two pieces instead of one. No doubt some customers are tedious, but an observant, thoughtful salesman soon learns the character of a buyer and adapts him self to the circumstances. A dull, heavy salesman, who has one rule for all and no capacity for realising character, is a serious drawback to the business of the firm by which he is employed.

INSTANCES OF ABSENCE OF MIND.

We have been interested on two separate occasions by observing how possible it is for men's minds to be so absorbed in a particular study or pursuit as to shut out apparently the capacity of seeing the bearing or meaning of ordinary statements, when made by persons in their company.

On one occasion an eminent physician of this city called and asked us to show him the stock and arrangement of a Manchester home-trade house. We took him round the various departments, explaining certain matters pertaining to different classes of goods, and the value of the stock in particular rooms, and his almost invariable rejoinder was, "Yes, just so." When we had made our way back again to the starting-point, and were about to part company, he turned and said, "I am exceedingly obliged to you; I have been very much pleased to find that your rooms are on the whole well ventilated, windows being kept open in certain parts, and other arrangements made for the outlet of foul air." Not a word escaped his lips as to the size of the place, the character of the stock, or the number of assistants; the only thing that impressed him was the ventilation. We learned afterwards that this was a special point with him, and all his patients knew it well.

On another occasion two gentlemen visited us, one of them being a minister and the other a stock broker in this city. We were discussing certain matters affecting a gentleman of our acquaintance, when our friend the broker said, "There was no doubt that Mr. —— had become speculative, and it was a matter which gave him pain." "I am extremely sorry," said our reverend friend, "to hear your statement. I thought he was perfectly settled in his views and doctrine. I should not have gathered from conversation with him that he had any questioning in his mind." "Oh," said the broker, "I did not mean that he was speculative on theological points, but in shares, and I was afraid he would come to grief."

SOME PARTICULARS ANENT THE LONG FIRM.

The writer has often been tempted by customers to take presents, varying in character and value.

On one occasion a person had bought a somewhat large parcel of Irish linens. They were dispatched by van in the usual course to premises not far from Messrs. Westhead's factory, Brook Street. The guard delivered the goods, expecting to be paid as soon as they were checked, but when they had all been looked over and the book signed as correct in quantity, the man turned to the guard and said, "It is all right, I am going to pay on the last Friday." The guard said, "I was told it was a cash transaction, and I must take back either the goods or the money," and turning to the driver he told him to drive quickly back to the

P

warehouse and report his belief that mischief was meant. The writer immediately returned in the van, taking with him a big strong fellow called Dick, from the packing-room. When we arrived at the place and went in, the man at once said, "Now, this is all right ; you need have no fear; the account will be duly paid. Take this (which was a £5 note) for yourself, and tell your firm that the account is as safe as any on their books."

But one had only to look round the place and into the room adjoining, which was quite empty, to realise at once that we had some members of the long firm fraternity to deal with. The writer stepped to the door and said, "Dick, will you stand here ?" It was on the doorstep, so that the door could not be shut. We then turned to the man and said, "I am here to ask you for the money in payment of this invoice; failing that, I must take the goods back." He replied, "I cannot pay you to-day, and you shall not take the goods out of the place." Our only rejoinder was, "Dick, we must have these goods. Perhaps you will show this man into the back room." Dick stepped forward immediately, and the man was showing fight, but in a moment found himself on the floor. The two van men set to work, and whilst Dick was discussing matters in the next room all the goods were got out and into the van; that done, he joined us and away we went back to the warehouse.

It was a somewhat daring thing to do, and, unless the evidence of fraud is clear, it is a dangerous course to take.

Enquiries were made afterwards in the neighbourhood about the people, but they were a mystery to everybody; no one could give any intelligible account of them.

On another occasion, a member of the long firm took rooms in Cannon Street; he bought a few goods of the firm and wanted credit. In that case the guard saw that the room was empty with the exception of a stool and a basket, and brought the goods back, giving his opinion of the man and place. The writer went down and told the man he would be obliged to report him and the place to the trade society, and that he had better clear away. A few weeks afterwards the writer saw the same person in a cellar near Deansgate, his name printed on paper and pasted on the door. "Is that your name?" the writer asked. "Yes," he replied. "That is not the name you had on the door in Cannon Street a few weeks ago." He made some offensive remarks, and the writer answered, "If you are not away from here within twenty-four hours you will have a band of men here who will disturb you much, and your name and address will be known throughout business circles." The next day the door was found closed and no name appeared.

THE INSIDIOUSNESS OF BRIBING AND ITS RESULTING CONSEQUENCES.

If once a buyer for a house receives a bribe, whether in the form of entertainment, or money, or a present of any kind, and so in a measure puts himself in the power of the person from whom he buys, he immediately loses his independent footing and his self-respect, and is unable in future to do the best for his employer. The first present offered with a purpose is to be guarded against; safety and happiness depend upon its being fairly understood that the only reason one has for buying is the need of the goods.

CERTAIN PEOPLE WHO REQUIRE GOOD MEMORIES.

When listening to the palpable misstatements that are sometimes made in the very midst of protestations of good faith by a debtor at a meeting of creditors, the writer has more than once been reminded of the story of a judge, who had before him a man who did nothing but tell falsehoods, and when he was charged with it, said, " My lord, I have been wedded to truth from my infancy." " Yes, sir," said the judge, " but the question is, how long have you been a widower?"

We have found the knowledge of shorthand of very great service to us. Many times, when we have had conversations with customers about their position and their history with a view to opening a credit with the firm, we have taken down all their remarks and statements; and afterwards, perhaps two or three years afterwards, when we have had occasion to refer to their position again for purposes well known to principals in home-trade houses, we have read over to them then the statement taken down at the first interview, which was strangely at variance with the second setting forth of facts, and the debtor has looked more than curious when so confronted. The old statement is quite true, he who tells falsehoods should have a good memory.

PERSEVERANCE REWARDED.

A gentleman put a notice outside his door, "Wanted, a boy," instructing the applicants to apply at a certain place and time. A number of lads came, and as he did not know how to select one, he hit upon the plan to drive a nail into a tree, and said that the boy who could hit it with a stick from a given place three times in succession should have the place. Not one of them could do it; and he invited them all to come and try again the next day. However, only one came; the master let him try, and this time he managed to do it. The gentleman asked how it was that he was able to do it that day and not the day before. The boy answered, "I practised all yesterday; I was determined to try until I could do it, because my mother is so poor and I wanted to get the place that I might help her." His perseverance was rewarded.

SOME INTERESTING REFERENCES TO THE SPRING OR FOUNTAIN WHICH GAVE THE NAME TO FOUNTAIN STREET, MANCHESTER.

In the old records of the Manchester Court Leet it is stated there was one principal spring or fountain rising in what is now about the centre of the city, and from which the name of Fountain Street has been derived, which for a very long period—viz., from 1506 to 1776—continued to supply water to the inhabitants, being apparently, during a large portion of that period, almost the only public supply of that nature which existed.   In October, 1578, the Leet jury order that " No person shall take water from the conduit (as it was termed) in any vessel of greater value (capacity) than one woman is able to bear filled with water, and but one of every house at one time, and to have their cale (call or turn) as ath been accustomed." Acton's *Guide to Manchester*, 1804, says that on the occasion of the rejoicings for the coronation of Charles II., on the 23rd of April, 1661, after the authorities, inhabitants, troops, &c., had attended divine service at the Collegiate Church, the boroughreeve, constables, and the rest of the burgesses of the town not then in arms, accompanied Sir Ralph Assheton, knight and baronet, and divers neighbouring gentlemen of quality, together with the said warden and fellows of the said college, and divers other ministers, with the town musick playing before them upon loud instruments through the streets to the cross, and so forward to the conduit, officers and soldiers in their order.   The gentlemen and officers drank his majesty's health in claret, running forth at three streams of the said conduit, which was answered from the soldiers by a great volley of shot, and many great shouts, saying God save the king ! which being ended, the gentry and ministers went to dinner, attended with the officers and musick of the town, the auxiliaries dining at the same place. During the time of dinner and until after sunset the said conduit did run with pure claret, which was freely

drunk by all that could, for the crowd, come so near
the same."

RAINFALL AT AND SUPPLY OF WATER FROM THE RESERVOIRS OF THE MANCHESTER CORPORATION WATERWORKS.

Nothing in this connection, we are sure, would be
more gratifying to our late friend Alderman George
Booth, were he here amongst us, than the subjoined
quotation for general information from the statistics
relating to this subject which he had with such care
collected whilst occupying the position of deputy-
chairman of the waterworks committee of the Manchester Corporation. The figures are striking, and
must impress every thoughtful mind with the magnitude of the works in Longdendale and the reservoirs
from Godley to Prestwich, to which will shortly be
added Thirlmere, with its pure and almost limitless
supply of water. To contemplate a population of
over one million human beings within sight of a dearth
of one of the first necessities of life, one which is constantly needed for domestic purposes, to say nothing
of the collapse which must ensue of almost every
industry, and the sufferings of the animals in our
midst, is enough to appal the stoutest heart. We
believe that the citizens of Manchester feel with ourself
that over against occasional errors of judgment (and
who does not err) the Corporation of Manchester have
to be credited with a foresight and courage worthy of
all praise.

ANNUAL RAINFALL AT THE RESERVOIRS, 1855 TO 1878.

Year.	Prest-wich.	Gorton.	Den-ton.	Godley.	Arn-field.	Rhodes Wood.	Tor-side.	Wood-head.
	Inches.	Inches.	Inches.	Inches.	Inches.	Inches.	Inches.	Inches.
1855 ...	...	25·55	24·19	24·54	30·63	34·49	...	40·43
1856 ...	...	35·76	34·20	35·94	42·61	49·07	...	50·97
1857 ...	...	31·41	29·16	30·31	36·59	40·04	...	46·06
1858 ...	...	29·85	27·54	28·32	36·14	44·26	...	45·54
1859 ...	...	34·13	34·26	32·60	40·20	47·26	...	53·35
1860 ...	...	35·34	35·51	36·08	39·52	47·85	...	53·74
1861 ...	...	29·78	28·28	31·11	32·43	40·22	...	44·24
1862 ...	...	38·15	36·69	35·50	38·99	47·28	...	49·63
1863 ...	...	37·30	35·81	36·14	38·19	48·04	...	53·77
1864 ...	...	27·63	27·13	29·28	31·34	38·48	...	43·66
1865 ...	...	28·17	28·28	26·49	29·37	37·15	35·08	40·35
1866 ...	...	41·64	40·47	42·94	47·50	58·45	55·45	64·58
1867 ...	...	34·17	34·11	36·57	39·46	49·55	47·98	55·96
1868 ...	...	31·19	30·22	31·02	35·47	46·93	45·41	53·62
1869 ...	...	33·75	33·24	35·66	40·05	49·16	50·93	59·12
1870 ...	...	28·93	28·08	30·04	34·45	39·88	40·16	46·62
1871 ...	...	29·58	29·16	31·45	33·88	38·99	38·27	43·73
1872 ...	...	48·01	48·18	49·47	52·70	59·25	59·48	64·31
1873 ...	33·05	27·99	27·30	29·28	35·58	37·66	38·62	41·14
1874 ...	36·94	30·47	30·47	30·83	39·34	42·53	43·59	46·67
1875 ...	40·10	32·53	31·41	32·17	38·35	40·73	43·87	45·89
1876 ...	40·20	35·42	35·32	37·85	44·84	46·85	49·18	51·61
1877 ...	47·39	44·14	43·64	43·48	54·07	57·05	60·35	63·44
1878 ...	35·36	33·64	32·64	32·71	41·01	42·54	44·36	47·39
Average	38·84	33·52	32·72	33·74	38·86	45·15	46·62	50·24

AREA, CAPACITY, AND DEPTH OF RESERVOIRS.

Name of Reservoir.	Area of Reservoir.	Capacity of Reservoir.	Depth of Reservoir.
	Acres.	Gallons.	Feet.
Woodhead	135	1,181,000,000	71
Torside	160	1,474,000,000	84
Rhodes Wood	54	500,000,000	68
Vale House	63	343,000,000	40
Bottoms	50	407,000,000	48
Arnfield	39	209,000,000	52
Hollingworth...	13	73,000,000	52
Godley	15	61,000,000	21
Denton, No. 1	7	30,000,000	20
Denton, No. 2	6	23,000,000	20
Gorton, Upper	34	123,000,000	26
Gorton, Lower	23	100,000,000	29
Prestwich	4½	20,000,000	22
	603½	4,544,000,000	
Reservoirs in course of construction at Audenshaw and Denton (estimated).	372	1,860,000,000	
	975½	6,404,000,000	

The average daily supply from the Corporation Waterworks has been increasing at the following rate :—

						Average supply per day.
In the year 1855	...	...	...	...	...	8,078,152
,, 1865	...	...	...	...	...	11,156,433
,, 1875	...	...	...	...	...	17,133,434
,, 1885	...	...	...	...	...	19,215,657
,, 1888	...	...	...	...	...	19,360,880

Since 1884 the largest daily averages have been reached in the months of May, June, July, August; and the lowest in the month of January.

DEVELOPMENT OF THE RAILWAY SYSTEM OF THE UNITED KINGDOM BETWEEN 1854 AND 1888 INCLUSIVE.

The Railway Returns of Capital and Traffic issued by the Board of Trade show the development of railway business over a period of thirty-five years. Within this time the length of lines opened for traffic has increased from 8,053 to 19,812 miles, the paid-up capital has risen from £286,000,000 to nearly £865,000,000, the number of passengers conveyed has increased from 111,000,000 to 742,000,000, and the gross receipts of the companies, which amounted to about £21,000,000 in 1854, have grown to £73,000,000 in 1888.

If the results shown by the returns for 1888 are compared with the returns of the years more immediately preceding, it appears that the financial improvement noted in the last report has been more than maintained; this is especially true of goods traffic, the gross receipts from which show an increase of $3\frac{3}{4}$ per cent, against an increase from 1886 to 1887 of $2\frac{1}{2}$ per cent. Accordingly, despite new investments of some magnitude, the average rate of dividend paid on ordinary capital rose to 4·22 per cent from 4·08 in 1887, and 3·94 in 1886. In 1888 the total paid-up capital of the railway companies of the United Kingdom was increased by £18,724,000, a larger increase on the capital of the previous year than has taken place in any of the last ten years except 1882 (when the increase was £22,372,000), as will be seen from the subjoined table :—

Year.	Amount of Capital.	Increase.
1879	... ... £717,003,000	... ... £18,458,000
1880	 728,317,000	 11,314,000
1881	 745,528,000	 17,211,000
1882	 767,900,000	 22,372,000
1883	 784,921,000	 17,021,000
1884	 801,464,000	 16,543,000
1885	 815,858,000	 14,394,000
1886	 828,344,000	 12,486,000
1887	 845,972,000	 17,628,000
1888	 864,696,000	 18,724,000

This amount, £18,724,000, represents an addition of about 2½ per cent to the capital paid up at the end of 1887, and is made up of about £11,500,000 added to the capital of English companies, nearly £7,200,000 to the capital of the Scotch, and a small amount, £82,000 only, to the capital of the Irish companies.

The amounts of each class of capital paid up at the end of 1888 were: Ordinary capital, £322,338,446; loans and debenture stock, £218,852,698; and guaranteed and preferential capital, £323,504,819; bearing respectively the proportions of 37, 25, and 38 per cent to the total paid-up capital.

SUCCESSION DUTY.

On every succession, according to the value thereof:—

To the lineal issue or lineal ancestor of the
predecessor ... ... 1 per cent.
To a brother or sister or any descendant... 3 „
To an uncle or aunt or any descendant ... 5 „
To a great uncle or aunt or any descendant 6 „
To any other relation or to a stranger in
blood ... ... 10 „

Where personal property in the United Kingdom is given by the will of a person dying domiciled abroad succession duty is not payable. "It is quite clear that you cannot apply an English Act of Parliament to foreign property while it remains foreign property; but after the purposes of administration have been answered and distribution made, if a party taking this distributive part comes to this country and invests it upon trusts, it assumes the character of a British settlement and British property."—Per Lord Westbury.

EXEMPTIONS.

Where the whole succession or successions derived from the same predecessor, and passing upon death to any person or persons, shall not amount in money or principal value to £100.

Any succession which, as estimated according to the provisions of the Succession Duty Act, is of less than £20 in the whole.

Any moneys applied to the payment of the duty on any succession according to any trust for that purpose.

Any succession which, if it were a legacy bequeathed to the successors by the predecessor, would be exempted from legacy duty.

Any property subject to legacy duty.

INLAND POSTAGE RATES.

LETTERS, BOOKS, AND PARCELS.

Weight not exceeding lb. oz.	Letter post. d.		Book post. d.	Weight. lb.	Parcels.			Charge. s. d.	
0 1	1	...	½	1	...	...	...	0	3
0 2	1½	...	½	2	...	...	...	0	4½
0 4	2	...	1	3	...	...	...	0	6
0 6	2½	...	1½	4	...	...	...	0	7½
0 8	3	...	2	5	...	...	...	0	9
0 10	3½	...	2½	6	...	...	...	0	10½
0 12	4	...	3	7	...	...	...	1	0
0 14	and ½d.		and ½d.	8	...	...	...	1	1½
1 0	for every		for every	9	...	...	..	1	3
1 2	additional		additional	10	...	...	...	1	4½
1 4	2 ounces.		2 ounces.	11	...	...	...	1	6

THINGS NOT TO BE DONE OR SAID.

Don't trust to chance.

Don't trust to the spur of the occasion. James Garfield, the late President of the United States, said—

" That trust is vain. Occasions cannot make spurs; if you expect to wear spurs, you must win them; if you wish to use them, you must buckle them to your feet before going into the fight."

Don't trust even to friends when financial responsibilities are upon you.

Don't buy without a fair prospect of being able to pay.

Don't spend what is not your own.

Don't crush out of your turn when getting a ticket at a station or place of amusement.

Don't allow your moral standard to be lowered when visiting a watering place.

Don't forget to insure your life when young when the premiums are low.

Don't forget to allow your attention to be given to the reduction of your premiums so that as you advance in life your payments may be small or absolutely cleared.

Don't forget that in a place of business the saving which may be effected in little things, such as twine and paper, is very great.

Don't forget in saving for your employer you will be helping yourself in more ways than one.

Don't forget to be cautious in what you say when selling goods to a buyer much older than yourself; he knows from experience many things you have not yet learned.

Don't forget that the man who lies is a fool, and is sure to be found out some day.

Don't forget what a well-known Lancashire man is

reputed to have said, "Honesty is the best policy, for I have tried both."

Don't forget that if you are not up to time with your new patterns some one will be before you and pick up the worms you might have had.

Don't forget that a man is not true to his high calling and capability who seeks to live on another man's earnings. The Bishop said, "A man cannot use that portion of the Lord's Prayer, 'give me day by day my daily bread,' when he is trying to get another man's bread."

Don't gamble at a bazaar ; much mischief is often caused by this.

Don't be a tale-bearer, but draw the distinction intelligently between this and reporting in a proper spirit what you know to be going wrong ; don't allow your employer to suffer loss when you can prevent it.

Don't be easily offended ; some people are thoughtless. Cowper said, "A moral, sensible, well-bred man will not affront me, and no other can."

Don't box a child's ears. It often leads to a lifelong deafness, greatly marring and sometimes almost ruining the prospects of later life.

Don't use big words. Remember John Bright's style ; words of one or two syllables are far more effective.

Don't forget that the strength of life is in the power of each little common act.

Don't forget the good that will be realised if you associate occasionally with men older than yourself; you will learn that things you thought new are old and well known, and you will form a little less estimate of your own capacities.

Don't, above all, be conceited in your notions and habits of dress and speech. Be simple.

Don't try to attract notice by your special mode of laughter or loud mode of speech.

Don't speak offensively to those under your control or "lord it" over them.

Don't try to pick out every little fault in people you occasionally meet; seek the good parts.

Don't talk for the sake of talking. Remember the four ingredients Sir William Temple said there should be in all conversation—truth, good sense, good humour, and wit.

Don't forget that you should treat *all* women with respect.

Don't forget that reading impure literature is taking poison into your own moral nature.

Don't forget that the use of indecent language is bad, whether by men or women, and especially in the hearing of children.

Don't forget that a kind word is a powerful word.

Don't forget that kindness is due to domestic animals, and to all God's creatures.

Don't forget the old saying that "one hour in bed before midnight is worth two afterwards."

Don't forget that a man who cannot mind his own business is not a safe one to be entrusted with another's.

Don't forget that every day well and truly lived makes the morrow more hopeful.

ANENT APPLICATIONS FOR SITUATIONS.

We have often been amused at the different ways and methods of approach, and the peculiar combination of words made use of when men and youths apply for situations.

One man will come in and say, " Have you such a thing as a situation to give away?" Our reply, " We don't give things away here." "Oh, I mean do you keep situations like?" "No," we again reply, "these are *sale* rooms, we don't *keep* things; will you please put your enquiry in some more definite form?" He then says, "Well, have you any work that will suit me, I want a place." "Now we see your object, we have nothing suitable at present, call again some other day."

Another comes, and in an awkward way asks, " Do you find situations here?" " No, we don't." " Then you have nothing to give away." " No, not at present."

There seems to be some misunderstanding about the meaning of the word situation, which is the cause of much confusion in the minds of many good honest work-fellows who are seeking such.

We were very much amused on one occasion when a stylish young gentleman called and said, "I have come down from —— and am anxious to know if it be possible for me to recommend myself to your notice with a view to an appointment or engagement, as buyer for your —— department, or almost any fancy department; I have had large experience in the fancy trade." The reply was, "We are obliged to you for the call, but the recommendation cannot be effective, as we have no immediate prospect of an opening likely to suit you."

ACCIDENTS ON THE BRITISH RAILWAYS IN 1888.

The total number of persons, who have been killed during the year 1888, is 905, and the number of injured 3,826.

Of the above numbers, 107 persons killed and 1,408 persons injured were passengers; but of these only 11 were killed and 594 injured in consequence of accidents to or collisions between trains; the deaths of the remaining 96 passengers and the injuries to 814 being returned as due to a variety of other causes, and especially to want of caution on the part of the individuals themselves.

Of the remainder, 396 killed and 2,193 injured were officers or servants of the railway companies or contractors.

Of suicides there were 65; of trespassers 230 were killed and 114 injured; of persons passing over the railway at level crossings, 53 were killed and 24 injured; and from miscellaneous causes, 54 persons were killed and 87 injured.

In addition to the above, the companies have returned 72 persons killed and 4,981 injured from accidents on their premises, not connected with the movement of railway vehicles.

The total number of passenger journeys, exclusive of journeys by season-ticket holders, was, in round numbers, 742,830,000 for the year 1888, or 9,160,000 more than in the previous year. Calculated on these figures, the proportions of passengers killed and injured during the year, from all causes, were 1 in 6,942,336 killed, and 1 in 527,577 injured. In 1887 the proportions were 1 in 6,064,000 killed, and 1 in 565,667 injured.—*From the General Report to the Board of Trade.*

THE INCOME-TAX ACT, 1853, 16 AND 17 VICTORIA, CAP. 34.

An Act for granting to her Majesty duties on profits arising from property, possessions, trades, and offices.

For the purpose of classifying and distinguishing the several properties, profits, and gains, or in respect of which the said duties are by this Act granted, and for the purpose of the provisions for assessing, raising,

Q

levying, and collecting such duties respectively, the said duties shall be deemed to be granted and made payable yearly for and in respect of the several properties, profits, and gains respectively described or comprised in the several schedules contained in this Act, and to be charged under such respective schedules.

Schedule A.

For and in respect of the property in all lands, tenements, hereditaments and heritages in the United Kingdom, and to be charged for every twenty shillings of the annual value thereof.

In collecting taxes on warehouse, shop, or house property the collector demands the tax upon the rackrent, irrespective of expenses incurred for repairs, alterations, or improvements, although the latter may enhance the value of the property, and so increase the rent and the amount of the tax collectable for ensuing years; to use the words of the Act, the property owner is to be called upon to pay the tax upon every twenty shillings of annual value.

Why should a person be called upon to pay taxes upon an income which only appears on paper and never comes into his possession? In business life this question often comes up for discussion. The writer has never been able to get or give a satisfactory answer.

It is possible for one to give a balance sheet as correct of his property account as it is of his business, and the authorities have as great facility for discovering fraud or irregularity in one as in the other. Why, then, should there be a different law for the two separate classes of accounts?

The writer does not demur to the payment of a reasonable income-tax; the government of the country necessitates large expenditure, and every one ought in his degree and capacity to contribute to that expenditure, but to pay a tax on £100 when one only receives

£30 or £60 is unjust and contrary to the ordinary law which guides all commercial operations, and at the same time stifles enterprise and energy.

EXEMPTIONS FROM RATES AND TAXES IN ENGLAND.

The following series of questions and answers on the subject of taxation are worthy of careful attention:—

The Chancellor of the Exchequer has just given an important and interesting body of answers to a series of questions addressed to him on the subject of the privilege of exemption from rates and taxes in this country. These answers are the result of questions submitted by the Chancellor to the various Government officials concerned on the subject. The matter originated in an enquiry or series of enquiries sent over to this country by a committee in Toronto, Canada. We append the questions and answers in their order:—

1. Does the Government of England pay local taxes to the municipalities in which it holds properties? If not, does it contribute anything in lieu of rates towards paying the expenses for making and maintaining the streets, for fire and police protection, or any other expenses for the good government of such municipalities wherein the Government holds properties for national purposes? If so, to what extent and upon what principles?

Answer: By English law property occupied for the public service is exempt from all local taxation. The English Government, however, determined in the year 1874 that all property in its occupation should from that date bear its fair share of the local burdens in the parishes and places in which it is situated; and for the purpose of its contributions to the rates, the Government has caused all its property to be valued. Upon the valuations so made, contributions in lieu of rates are paid by way of poundage out of an annual vote of Parliament. The contributions are calculated upon the rateable value of the Government property, according to the poundage rate of the rates levied in the parishes and places in which it is situated.

2. Are churches and church property by law exempt from local taxation?

Answer: Churches are exempt, but not church property, which is liable to local taxation like other property.

3. Are universities, denominational colleges, church schools, and other places of learning and charitable institutions by law exempt from local taxation?

Answer: No; it was decided by the House of Lords a few years ago, in the Mersey Docks case, that property in the occupation of institutions of this kind was not entitled to exemption, but was rateable like other property.

4. Are judges, law and Government officials in England by law exempt on their official incomes from local and national taxation?

Answer: Property in the occupation of the Crown, including Government in all its branches as well as the sovereign, is exempt from local taxation; and incomes, whether official or otherwise, are not liable in any case to be assessed to local taxation. The income-tax is confined to the imperial revenue, and there is no exemption for these official incomes. Note: The only British official who is exempt from income-tax by law is the sovereign; but the present sovereign, though exempt, voluntarily pays it.

5. Are clergymen of any denomination in England by law exempt on the houses they live in, and on their incomes from local and national taxation?

Answer: They are not exempt as to their houses, and they are not exempt as to their incomes. (See answer to No. 4.)

6. Are the members of the English Government, such as the Lord Chancellor, Premier, and others, holding offices of high position in the English Cabinet, by law exempt from paying taxes on their official incomes, either local or national?

As to their incomes there is no exemption. (See answers 4 and 5.)

THE GROWTH OF CANADA.

One of the Dominion ministers, speaking the other day, presented one or two striking proofs of the growth and general prosperity of the country.

Taking first the money of the people he found this to be true:

Deposits in the chartered banks had increased from \$77,891,000 in 1879 to \$123,655,000 in 1889, and deposits in the savings banks from \$24,128,000 to \$71,022,000 in the same period. As to the railways in Canada, this year, 1889, there are 12,701 miles of line open as against 6,255 miles in 1879. In 1879 there were 6,523,000 passengers carried and 11,416,000 in 1888; while the tons of freight increased in the same period from 8,348,000 to 17,172,000.

There could be no better indication of increasing population and commercial development, and it is as gratifying to us at home as it is to our brethren in the new country. Continued prosperity to them is our desire, and we wish equal prosperity and development to our friends in Newfoundland and in British Columbia.

THE RELATION OF THE PRESENT TO THE FUTURE.

We have been frequently struck with the force of ideas suggesting every man's duty to the future of his family and of the race. A passage in the book of inspired wisdom says: " Instead of thy fathers shall be thy children, whom thou shalt make princes in all the earth." The meaning obviously is that men, instead of glorying in their ancestors, should give their thoughts and affections and consecrate their powers to their children, that they shall stand out as strong and true— as princes in the earth. Much of the question as to the relation of the present to the future depends, in accordance with the recently emphasized laws of heredity and environment and their application to social and moral life, upon the character transmitted and training given by parent to child. We glory in our fathers because of the progress that has been made.

The former days were days of evil, of dirt, of oppression, and of comparative starvation. We to-day enjoy the results of the progress that has been made. Knowledge and intelligence have accumulated; the food of the working-man to-day was the food of nobles a hundred years ago—indeed, the salads of those days would not be eaten by our people now; and meat, which thirty years ago was a dainty rarely seen and more rarely tasted by the less wealthy classes, is now the daily food in most families. Our corporations and our national assembly regard the housing of the poor ; the health of the lowly is attracting the attention of our leaders and nobles, and the dirt and squalor of the eighteenth century, nay, of forty years ago, would not now be tolerated a single day. It is for us to say whether our sons shall make their influence felt on the period in which they live. Never were the opportunities greater. The future is largely in the people's hands, because the power is more and more so; every man of intelligence and energy can write his name on the sands of this time. The life of commerce is one of the greatest civilising forces of the world, lifting men up by its increased demands upon them to higher levels of thought and action, and making them more than ever conscious of their moral responsibilities. Never before did there go forth such evidences of generosity and philanthropy, all of which are the outcome of moral force inspired by divine power. Shall we not so direct our energies as to still further mellow and shape for good the intellectual capacities that are strengthening around us on every side, treating our children, not as dolls, but as beings capable of a great work in this world and a noble inheritance in the greater future world?

PUBLIC COMPANIES.

Mr. Thomas Skinner says the following figures show the recent rate of company forming under the Limited Liability Acts:—

	No. of companies registered.	Registered capital.
1887	2,051	£170,172,674
1886	1,891	145,850,702
1885	1,482	119,222,961
1884	1,541	138,491,428
1883	1,766	167,680,187
1882	1,632	254,744,331
1881	1,581	210,711,657
1880	1,302	168,466,322
1879	1,034	75,568,047
1878	886	67,856,975

The number of companies actually existing, with the total paid-up capital, is as follows:—

	No. of companies existing at date.	Total paid-up capital at date.
April, 1888	11,001	£611,430,371
„ 1887	10,894	591,508,692
„ 1886	9,471	529,637,684
„ 1885	9,320	494,909,862
„ 1884	8,641	475,551,294

The Local Government Board gives the total local indebtedness of the country at £186,221,642, which is borrowed at rates varying from 2¾ to 4 per cent per annum.

RYLANDS MEMORIAL CLUB.

In April, 1889, the writer was present at a meeting of the directors, buyers, and salesmen of the firm of Rylands and Sons Limited, convened for the purpose of founding the Rylands Memorial Club, to perpetuate the memory of the late head of the firm, Mr. John Rylands. It was felt that there could be no more effective way of accomplishing this than by founding a social club, as a means of knitting together in friendly intercourse, and for purposes of mutual improvement, self-help, and entertainment, those whom the late Mr. Rylands had, by his great power as a leader and man of business, united in the common interests of commercial life. Already a fire brigade, trained and ready for service, a band, and a dramatic and orchestral society have been established in connection with the club.

SCRAPS.

The writer remembers once calling upon a well-known banker in the city. After the conversation upon the subject of the visit was concluded, the gentleman said, putting his hand upon the shoulder of the writer, " Do you make any bad debts at your place ?" " Yes," we replied, " we do occasionally, and we would not give much for a firm which did not at times do so; such would appear to us wanting in enterprise and courage."

To which he responded, " I am pleased to hear your opinion; it is exactly in accord with my own; no growing business can be conducted without now and again making a mistake; we must run some risks."

———

Amiability is very good, but it is a grace that needs to be allied with strong principle, lest in seeking as it does to please all, it be led by flattery to smile on wrong.

———

We remember reading of Mr. Ledyard, the great traveller, at the time he was brought before the Geographical Society of Great Britain; they wanted him to make some explorations in Africa, and having told him some of the dangerous parts of the work, they asked him how soon he could go. His reply was, "To-morrow morning." How different his reply to that which is often given by some of our young men, when asked to do certain things or go to some new place. They wonder what will happen, and want to discuss whether they are the most suitable men, and a host of difficulties are raised that thwart and destroy the good intention one had of helping them on to higher and better duties.

———

Lord Lawrence said it was only the love he had for an invalid sister that kept him at school and close to his studies. He worked hard, and every prize he won he took home and laid it in her lap as a token of his love; and so he improved and enlarged his mind and powers of administration, and eventually became Viceroy of India. What are the words of this good man about our missionaries? They are worth quoting. "Notwithstanding all that the English people have done to benefit India, the missionaries have done more than all other agencies combined."

It is well to remember the old proverb, "Bear with a hen's cackle for the sake of the eggs;" in other words, little annoyances must be put up with for the sake of great advantages.

"Health," one writer says, "energetic health is more to be desired than talent or genius. A pound of energy with one ounce of talent will achieve greater results than a pound of talent with one ounce of energy."

God has so constituted us that in doing good we make ourselves the recipients of good.

In the providence of God, courses of action present themselves as duties which we often think we are not qualified to perform, and we shrink from the responsibility. Dare to fail; help is near at hand, if your heart is right, and you know where to seek it.

APPENDIX.

BRITISH RAILWAYS.	Capital Issued.	Par Price.	Mileage. 1888.	Prices. Hst.	Prices. Date.
	£		Miles.		
Caledonian Ordinary	39,607,241	100	791	118¾	Dec. 27
Ditto Con. Guar. Pref. 4 per cent...	... ...	...	...	126¾	Sep. 19
Ditto Debentures	... ...	...	...	131¼	July 18
East London	5,790,265	100	...	12⅝	Nov. 15
Furness Ordinary	... ...	100	139	106¾	Jan. 18
Ditto Debentures 4 per cent... ...	... ...	...	...	127¼	April 9
Glasgow and South-Western	14,016,746	100	348	109¾	Sep. 20
Great Eastern Ordinary	44,083,437	100	1,082	72¼	Sep. 26
Ditto Con. Irred. Pref. 4 per cent	... ...	...	...	126½	April 6
Great Northern	28,642,077	100	977	120½	April 12
Ditto " A "	... ...	...	...	106¼	Jan. 10
Great North of Scotland Ordinary	5,326,406	100	315	60⅞	Oct. 18
Great Western	72,493,466	100	2,469	152⅛	Sep. 27
Ditto Rent Chrg. Guar. 5 per cent	... ...	...	...	158¾	July 23
Ditto Consold. Guar. 5 per cent ...	... ...	...	...	158¾	July 13
Ditto Debentures	... ...	...	...	134	Mar. 16
Lancashire and Yorkshire	43,637,362	100	524	121¾	Jan. 11
London and Brighton Ordinary	23,993,731	100	476	145	Oct. 3
Ditto Preferred	... ...	...	...	161	July 25
Ditto Deferred	... ...	...	...	133¾	Sep. 26
Ditto 5 per cent Cons. Guar. ...	... ...	...	...	155	Oct. 27
London, Chatham, and Dover Ordinary ...	26,693,481	100	180	25	Sep. 27
Ditto Contgt. Pref. 4½ per cent ...	... ...	...	...	103¾	Sep. 26
London and North-Western	101,908,328	100	1,875	173¼	Dec. 31
Ditto 4 per cent Con. Guar.	... ...	...	...	129¾	Mar. 19
Ditto 4 per cent Debentures	... ...	...	...	135	Mar. 14
London and South-Western	31,038,855	100	878	143¾	Dec. 15

1888.		Prices. 1887.		Prices. 1886.		Prices. 1885.		Prices. 1884.		Prices. 1883.	
Lst.	Date.	Hst.	Lst.	Hst.	Lst.	Hst.	Lst.	Hst.	Lst.	Hst.	Lst.
99½	June 14	105	93½	105⅛	96¼	103⅝	90⅞	103⅞	92	110¾	100⅜
119½	Jan. 10	118¼	111½	114⅝	111	114	107	114	106½	108½	105⅛
120½	Jan. 3	120½	116	117⅝	114	117	108½	120	109¼	111½	108
8½	June 18	13¾	7½	17⅜	8	17	9¾	24¾	17¼	26½	19
92¼	June 15	108	88¼	106½	86¼	107	98½	118	105½	149	118½
117¾	Jan. 7	118⅝	112½	116	113	117	111¼	118½	108¾	112¾	109
98½	May 4	103½	97½	104	95¼	110½	91½	117¾	107	123¼	114¼
63¾	Mar. 8	70⅝	64¼	74¼	62½	69¼	57⅞	69¼	56⅞	78	60⅞
115¾	Feb. 4	117⅞	111	116	111	113½	106½	113¾	106	109⅝	105
111	Feb. 29	116¼	110½	117¾	108	114½	104½	116	109	124¾	111½
96½	Mar. 6	109	96½	113¼	102	106⅝	92½	112	95½	134½	107¼
52	April 24	60½	53¼	59¼	46¾	54⅜	44	56	40¼	59½	50⅝
138⅝	Mar. 8	140½	132⅞	139⅞	126½	140⅞	124⅞	145⅝	132⅝	148½	132¾
148	Jan. 3	148½	140½	145	140¼	144	133	143½	134½	137¼	132
148¼	Jan. 3	148½	140	145¼	139½	143¾	132½	144¼	134½	136⅞	132
124	Jan. 3	126¾	118⅜	124½	118¾	122¾	113	126¾	113½	116¾	111
113¾	Mar. 1	123	113½	115¼	99¼	117½	104¼	118⅜	111¾	132⅝	109
135	Mar. 8	137	125	133	115¼	120	105	122	112	129¾	116½
152	Feb. 2	154	143	150½	139½	142	130	140¾	128	142	134
111⅞	Mar. 9	122¾	106⅝	119¾	93⅜	104⅞	79	108⅝	89⅞	122⅞	99⅜
144¼	Feb. 2	145¾	137	140½	136	138¾	130¼	140	131¼	136	130
19¾	Mar. 8	25⅛	19¾	26¾	18⅛	20¼	13¼	24¼	17¾	29¼	22
95¼	Mar. 8	102⅝	95¼	103⅜	87½	98	73½	106⅛	94	106¾	100¼
163	Mar. 8	169¼	160	167	151½	170¾	153⅝	174	162¾	178⅞	169½
121¾	Jan. 6	122	115½	119¾	115¼	119½	109½	119½	111¼	114½	112½
126¾	Feb. 14	128½	118	124	119	124¾	114	127	114	116⅞	112¼
131	Jan. 3	133	123½	128¾	118¼	129½	119½	131½	122¾	136	128

BRITISH RAILWAYS.	Capital Issued.	Par Price.	Mile-age. 1888.	Prices. Hst.	Prices. Date.
	£		Miles.		
Manchester, Sheffield, and Lincolnshire ...	26,638,474	100	287	73¾	Jan. 11
Ditto Preferred	... ...	...	...	109½	Jan. 12
Ditto Deferred	... ...	...	...	40	Sep. 15
Metropolitan Consolidated	14,292,857	100	35	77¾	Dec. 27
Ditto Surplus Lands	... ...	...	...	72⅜	April 4
Metropolitan District	8,214,019	100	13	37	Jan. 13
Ditto 5 per cent Contingent Pref....	... ...	...	...	69½	Jan. 7
Midland	82,046,856	100	1,296	136½	Dec. 31
Ditto 4 per cent Perp. Pref. Stk....	... ...	...	...	128½	Aug. 15
Ditto 4 per cent Debentures	... ...	...	...	134	Mar. 13
North British Ordinary...	42,460,242	100	1,033	131½	Sep. 25
Ditto E. and G. Ordinary	... ...	...	...	54½	Sep. 26
Ditto Ordinary Pref.	... ...	...	...	77⅜	Sep. —
Ditto Ordinary	... ...	..	...	56½	Dec. 27
Ditto Con. Pref. No. 2 4 per cent...	... ...	...	...	122	Mar. 26
Ditto E. and G. Con. Pref. 4½ p. c.	... ...	...	...	133¾	Mar. 21
North-Eastern "Consols"	58,159,853	100	1,578	163½	Dec. 31
North Staffordshire	7,917,292	100	...	114	Aug. 18
Rhymney	1,534,017	100	...	204	Nov. 22
South-Eastern	22,461,935	100	...	134½	Sep. 21
Ditto Preferred	... ...	...	...	161	Sep. 29
Ditto Deferred	... ...	...	...	114⅜	Oct. 1
Ditto 5 per cent Prf. Contng. ..	... ...	...	...	153⅜	Mar. 29

888.		Prices. 1887.		Prices. 1886.		Prices. 1885.		Prices. 1884.		Prices. 1883.	
Lst.	Date.	Hst.	Lst.	Hst.	Lst.	Hst.	Lst.	Hst.	Lst.	Hst.	Lst.
66	May 31	77½	65	71	62¼	74½	63	83⅞	73	92⅝	81
99	Nov. 23	115¼	97	103¾	90	112¼	96	124¼	110	129¼	121¼
33	May 26	44¼	33½	41	32⅞	39	29	45⅞	34½	55⅜	44⅞
64	Mar. 7	72	62⅛	...	...	...	...	...	...	...	...
65½	Mar. 7	75	64¾	...	...	...	...	...	...	...	...
29⅜	Mar. 8	43¼	33¼	44½	37	60½	36⅞	72¼	55½	62½	51½
52	April 16	87	62½	90	76½	123	80	126¾	111	115¼	109
124⅝	Mar. 9	129⅝	121⅝	131½	122⅜	134¾	125½	137	129¼	140¼	131
117⅞	Jan. 3.	119	111½	116	111	...	...	...	...	...	...
124	Jan. 3.	127	118½	123¾	118½	122¾	113½	127	113¼	115¾	111¼
104⅛	Jan. 20	106⅜	96⅜	97⅞	87¼	97⅛	83¼	106½	91¾	106½	97
36½	April 18	38¼	32⅜	32¾	28	35½	26⅞	41¼	34¼	42¼	37⅛
71¾	Sep. —	...	...	...	...	...	...	...	...	...	...
44¾	Sep. —	...	...	...	...	...	...	...	...	...	...
115	Jan. 9	115	108	111½	107	109¼	102	109	103	105	100
127	Jan. 5	126½	118½	120½	117	118½	112	119	113½	115	111
149¾	May 17	158⅝	149¼	159¾	142⅛	160	142¾	171½	153¾	175⅞	165½
99½	Jan. 5	100½	90¾	94¼	88¾	92¾	81½	92¼	86	93¼	83
150½	Mar. 12	182	150	191½	180	190	133	191	152	180	174½
124¼	Feb. 9	132	124	130½	117	123	110	128½	119	132½	121
150	Jan. 31	155	147	152	143	146	137	147½	137½	147	140
98	Mar. 8	113⅜	97½	114	92⅜	101½	77⅝	111¾	95⅞	122½	108⅛
142	Jan. 9	143¾	136¾	139¾	135¼	139	131	140	131	154	129½

INDEX.

R

ERRATUM.

Page 7, line 2, for "seventeenth" read "eighteenth."